Understanding *(and Teaching)* the United States Constitution

Catherine McGrew Jaime

Other Books by Catherine Jaime:

Understanding the Electoral College
Simply Put: Economics
A Trial of a Trial (a Mock Trial Story)
Sharing Shakespeare with Students
The Rocky Road to Civil Rights in the United States
York Proceeded On: The Lewis and Clark Expedition Told Through the Eyes of Its Forgotten Member
Da Vinci: His Life and His Legacy
Doing Da Vinci for Kids

Creative Learning Connection
8006 Old Madison Pike
Madison, AL 35758

www.CreativeLearningConnection.com

© Catherine McGrew Jaime, 2011

Permission is granted to copy any portions of this book for use with **one** teacher's students. Please contact the author at cmmjaime@alum.mit.edu for additional licensing options.

Table of Contents

Notes & Quotes on the Constitution 4
Notes on Teaching the U.S. Constitution 5
Notes on the Influences of Scripture 6
Notes on the Ancient Greek Form(s) of Government & Republic of Rome's Form of Government 7
Notes on Other Influences on the U.S. Constitution 9
Notes on the Articles of Confederation, the First Constitution of the United States 10
Notes on the U.S. Constitution 11
Notes on the Ratifying Process and Notes on the Bill of Rights 14
Timeline of the U.S. Constitution 15
Using Constitution-Related Documents 32
What Say the Reeds at Runnymede? 34
The U.S. Constitution: Explanation of Articles 35
The Constitution of the United States (1787) 36
Magna Carta, (Originally signed in 1215) 76
The Mayflower Compact (1620) 79
Fundamental Orders of Connecticut (1639) 80
Massachusetts Body of Liberties, Excerpts from (1641) 81
English Bill of Rights (1689) 85
Resolutions of the Stamp Act (October 19, 1765) 88
Fairfax County Resolves (July 18, 1774) 90
Patrick Henry's Give Me Liberty or Give Me Death (1775) 99
Declaration of the Causes and Necessity of Taking Up Arms (July 6, 1775) 102
Thomas Paine's Common Sense, Excerpts from (January/February 1776) 109
Virginia Declaration of Rights (June 12, 1776) 114
The Constitution of Virginia (June 29, 1776) 117
Declaration of Independence (July 4, 1776) 120
The American Crisis I, Excerpt from (1776) 125
Pamphlet by Thomas Paine (December 23, 1776) 125
Articles of Confederation 126
The Northwest Ordinance (1787) 135
The Federalist Papers : No. 10 (Nov 23, 1787) 140
Danbury Baptist Association Letter and Thomas Jefferson's Response to Danbury Letter 148
Activities for Before and After Studying the Constitution 151

Notes on the Constitution

Too many people in the United States are ignorant of the foundational document of our country. I know I was for the first 40+ years of my life.

The Constitution itself is not long, and not particularly complicated. I carry a pocket version of it in my purse, and many of my students now carry them as well. (Ask for one the next time you visit your Senator or Congressman – most of them have copies available for the asking…)

But I believe that the history of the document is as important as the document itself, which is why I spend so much time here, and in my classes on its history.

Quotes on the Constitution

"The Constitution is the guide which I never will abandon." George Washington

"The U. S. Constitution doesn't guarantee happiness, only the pursuit of it. You have to catch up with it yourself." Benjamin Franklin

"Our Constitution was made only for a moral and religious people. It is wholly inadequate to the government of any other." John Adams

"The liberties of our country, the freedom of our civil constitution, are worth defending against all hazards: And it is our duty to defend them against all attacks." Samuel Adams

"The happy Union of these States is a wonder; their Constitution a miracle; their example the hope of Liberty throughout the world." James Madison

"We the people are the rightful masters of both Congress and the courts, not to overthrow the Constitution but to overthrow the men who pervert the Constitution." Abraham Lincoln

Notes on Teaching the U.S. Constitution

I have been a Government Club advisor for the last 12 years. During that time I have learned so much about the founding of our country and the workings of our government. Our Government Club participates in Youth Judicial (Mock Trial) competitions and Youth Legislature conferences every year. It was at a Legislature conference that I was first struck with the need to teach about the Constitution. During the weekend I heard numerous students discussing whether bills were constitutional or not – but it dawned on me that most of them had no idea what was in the Constitution!

From that experience came the first of many classes I have taught on the U.S. Constitution, and a seven-year stint as the advisor for the YMCA's Student Supreme Court.

I usually teach the Constitution in a weekly class, covering a semester's worth of work over the course of the school year. We spend the first half of the classes studying the history of the Constitution, including reading the many documents and about the many events that lead to the writing of the Constitution. After focusing on the history, we go through the Constitution itself – article by article, and amendment by amendment.

We spend most of the second half of the classes looking at important Supreme Court cases, and how the Constitution has been upheld (or not upheld) through the years by the various members of the Supreme Court.

This book deals with what we did in the first half of the year – the history of the Constitution and the Constitution itself. Everything you need to teach that portion is included here.

Whether you are planning to teach a class on the Constitution, or just want to fill in some gaps in your own learning, you should find this book to be helpful.

Notes on the Influences of Scripture

The founders knew the Bible; there is no question about that. Even those who did not consider themselves Christians knew the Bible well and respected it. Benjamin Franklin and Thomas Jefferson are usually included on any such list – though they both talked often of Divine Providence. There can be no doubt that the Scriptures influenced the men who wrote our founding documents, including the Constitution.

"What does the Lord require of you but to do justice, to love kindness, and to walk humbly with your God." Micah 6:8

"What does the Lord your God require of you but to fear the Lord your God, to walk in all his way and love Him, to serve the Lord your God with all your heart and with all your soul, and to observe the Lord's commandments." Deuteronomy 10:12-13

"It is I who judge uprightly. When the earth and all its people shake it is I who hold its pillars firm." Psalm 75:2

*"The law of the Lord is perfect, restoring the soul;
the testimony of the Lord is sure, making wise the simple.
The precepts of the Lord are right, rejoicing the heart;
The commandment of the Lord is radiant, enlightening the eyes.
The fear of the Lord is pure, enduring forever;
The judgements of the Lord are true;
They are righteous altogether."* Psalm 19:7-11

Notes on
the Ancient Greek Form(s) of Government
~750 – 500 B.C.

The Ancient Greeks were not united into one country, or under one central government. But rather, the different city-states ruled in their various locations and fashions. Some city-states were controlled by a tyrant, others were under a monarch, some an oligarchy, and some under a democracy.

"Democracy" = *"the rule of the people"* (The U.S. is **not** a democracy.")

Athens, for one, had a democracy (at least for the limited members of the society who had status as "citizens").

Socrates (a Greek philosopher about 400 years B.C.): "You obey the law simply because it's the law" (not because you might get caught).

Parthenon in Ancient Greece

"A pure democracy is a society consisting of a small number of citizens, who assemble and administer the government in person."
James Madison

Notes on
the Republic of Rome's Form of Government
509 - 27 B.C.

The Romans had a republic (as we do now). They emphasized separation of powers, and checks and balances.

"Republic" = *"representatives elected by the people to make the decisions for us"*

Julius Caesar's take on life (or government?): "Men willingly believe what they wish."

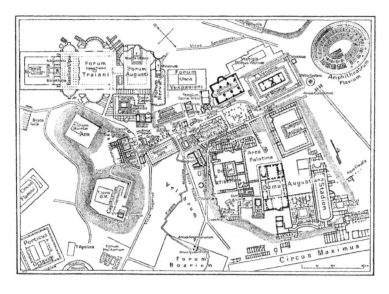

Map of Rome During the Republic of Rome

At the end of the Constitutional Convention of 1787, Benjamin Franklin was asked, *"Well, Doctor, what have we got, a republic or a monarchy?"* With no hesitation, Franklin responded, *"A republic, if you can keep it."*

**Notes on
Other Influences on the U.S. Constitution**

John Locke　　　　　*Montesquieu*　　　　*William Blackstone*

John Locke (English philosopher, living between 1632 and 1704) writes about his social contract theory, that God gives you certain rights when born, you enter into a government to assure those rights. His theory is well accepted by many who write our early political documents.

Montesquieu (a French political thinker, living between 1689 and 1755) writes his book, *The Spirit of the Law*. His idea of the separation of powers (checks and balances among three branches) influences our Founding Fathers.

William Blackstone (English judge and jurist between 1723 and 1780) writes his *Commentaries on the Laws of England*, which will become a foundation for law in America. Almost three centuries later, his works still stand as the classical view on the common law and its principles.

Notes on the Articles of Confederation, The First Constitution of the United States

Constitution = "a plan of government"
Confederation = "loose organization of states" (Central government-little power; states-most power)
Revolution = "a fast change" (can be violent or peaceful!)
Ratify = "approve"

Under the Articles of Confederation—states were in a <u>league of friendship.</u> Article II: *"Each state retains its sovereignty, freedom, and independence, and every power, jurisdiction, and right which is not by this confederation expressly delegated to the United States."*

Congress could declare war, make peace, borrow money, conduct foreign affairs, but it couldn't collect taxes! (States voluntarily contributed money, and sailors, and soldiers, if they so pleased!)

Each state had one vote (and nine were required to change anything)

The Federal Government lacked power to enforce treaties. (During this time, Great Britain refused to surrender forts in the Northwest and stirred up the Indians along our western borders. Britain was mad because the U.S. wasn't upholding its end of the treaty either. Britain and Spain were planning to split the spoils after the U.S. fell apart.)

John Adams went to Britain as a minister; they wanted to know where the other 12 ministers were! (Britain also refused to send a minister to the U.S.) The U.S. couldn't get trade treaties with other countries; and it was difficult to trade from state to state. Many states were raising taxes sharply, and many people were going to jail for their debts

Notes on the U.S. Constitution

"quorum" = "number that has to be present to conduct business"
"bicameral legislature" = "2 houses"
"compromise" = "people with 2 different positions, both agree to give a little, and meet in the middle"

The U.S. Constitution is the **oldest** and **shortest** living constitution in the world. All the mistakes had been made first time around (in Articles of Confederation), so got it right the second time around!

Many of us believe it is the best plan of government the world has seen.

We could definitely ask: "What was it about the time and place and people that got it right when it was written in 1787?"

Several answers could be given, including that:
- Some of the guys that worked on the first one, worked on the second one also!
- The Constitution equals a "bundle of compromises".

At the Philadelphia Convention, four things are decided immediately:
- Hold sessions in secret until done (to hold rumors at bay)
- Seven states equal a quorum, not the nine needed for Articles.
- Every state allowed one vote, regardless of delegates present.
- Only a simple majority required to make a decision (rather than 2/3 or 3/4)

This is about all they could agree on at the beginning!

It soon became obvious that they wouldn't be able to <u>fix</u> the articles, so they scrapped them and <u>started</u> over from scratch.

They knew right away it was going to be a long summer, to work out the problems:
- The central government needed more power, but how much more?
- The big states versus the little states
- Eliminate trade barriers between states (central government needed to "control trade" not individual states")
- Slavery

Interesting side note:
They made a practice of keeping someone with Benjamin Franklin when each session was over with, so he wouldn't accidentally blab what they were discussing….At the end of the convention, Benjamin Franklin commented on the chair with the sun on it. He stood up at the end and stated, "Gentlemen I believe now that that is a rising sun, not a setting sun." (In other words we are at the beginning, not the end, in creating this great nation.)

Bill of Rights:
Rhode Island didn't want to give up their freedoms, which led, with other things, to the Bill of Rights.

The first Congress started working on the Bill of Rights to spell out the freedoms that were implied.

Notes on the Ratifying Process

	Date Ratified:	# For:	# Against:
1. Delaware *("1st in Nation")*	12/7/1787	100%	
2. Pennsylvania	12/12/1787	46	23
3. New Jersey	12/18/1787	100%	
4. Georgia	1/2/1788	100%	
5. Connecticut	1/9/1788	128	40
6. Massachusetts	2/6/1788	187	168

(In Massachusetts, people like Sam Adams were against ratifying the Constitution because it had an executive branch, and too strong a central government.)

7. Maryland	2/6/1788	63	11
8. South Carolina	5/23/1788	149	73
9. New Hampshire	6/21/1788	57	46

(With ratification by these nine states, the Constitution goes into effect.)

10. Virginia	6/26/1788	89	79
11. New York	7/26/1788	30	27

(When G.W. is elected President only 11 states have joined the Union.)

12. North Carolina	11/21/1789	197	77
13. Rhode Island	5/29/1790	34	32

(Rhode Island was holding out for the promise of a Bill of Rights.)

Notes on the Bill of Rights

Views on Bill of Rights:

Anti-Federalists	**Federalists**
Want weak central government	Strong central government
Against ratification of the Constitution	In favor of the Constitution
For the Bill of Rights (Used to rally the Anti-Federalists)	Against the Bill of Rights

James Madison

Madison originally opposed the Bill of Rights, but promised to work for it when so many states requested it. (More than 200 amendments had been recommended by the states by this time – mainly to limit federal government or protect individual rights. Madison wasn't interested in the first kind, only the second kind.)

In March of 1789 Madison introduced 17 amendments to the House of Representatives, trying to please both the federalists and the anti-federalists. (One of his amendments that didn't pass would have kept states from violating the rights also.)

Madison wanted the amendments included **in** the constitution, **not** tacked onto the end.

In August the House would vote on the 12 amendments, and send them to the states for ratification.

In December the 9th state, Virginia, approved ten of the 12 amendments, which became the first ten amendments to the Constitution, or "the Bill of Rights".

Timeline of the U.S. Constitution

1215

The *Magna Carta* is signed by King John (The original is on display in the British Museum, a 1291 copy is on display in the U.S. National Archives.)

It includes two big promises:
1. The king won't be THE law, or ABOVE the law; will obey it like everyone else.
2. Some sort of governing body to determine taxes, besides the king.

1620

Mayflower Compact is signed by "Separatists and Strangers" who agree to follow all the laws when they make their new government.

1639

The Connecticut Council adopts the *Fundamental Orders of Connecticut*.

1641

The *Massachusetts Body of Liberties* is passed, containing 23 rights that make it into the U.S. Bill of Rights.

1689

The *English Bill of Rights* is signed.

1690s
John Locke, an English philosopher, writes his essays
on social contract theory.

1754
England and the American Colonies are at war against
the French, in the French and Indian War
(By 1756 it has spread to Europe as the "Seven Years War").

1760
George III becomes King of England.

1763
The French and Indian War ends – the expenses that have
piled up will now need to be paid with increased taxes.

Events in the Colonies leading up to War

1761
British Parliament passes *Writs of Assistance*—allowing
government officials to search anyone at any time
on the pretense of looking for smuggled goods.

April 1764
The Sugar Act is passed by the British Parliament, further taxing sugar, coffee, wines and other items coming into the colonies.

May 1764
In response to The Sugar Act, James Otis of Massachusetts complains of *"taxation without representation"*, and recommends boycotting British goods.

September 1764
The Currency Act is passed by the British Parliament, prohibiting the colonists from making their own paper money.

1765
William Blackstone writes his *Commentaries on the Laws of England*, which will become a foundation for law in America.

March 1765
The *Quartering Act* is passed by the British Parliament, requiring colonists to house and feed the British troops "protecting" them.

The Stamp Act is also passed by the British Parliament; the first direct tax on the colonists. It will tax legal documents, newspapers, dice, playing cards and much more in the colonies.

April 1765
Colonists get wind of *The Stamp Act*. They are outraged at the idea of Parliament taxing them, instead of letting them tax themselves. Riots occur throughout the colonies in response.

May 1765
Patrick Henry gives his speech to the Virginia Burgesses, and responds to cries of "treason" with:
"If this be treason, make the most of it…"

July 1765
Sam Adams helps create the *Sons of Liberty* in Massachusetts (a secret organization of colonists) to protest *The Stamp Act* and other recent actions by Parliament. Similar groups soon form in other colonies.

October 1765
The Stamp Act Congress meets in New York to discuss the colonies' reaction to the Stamp Act. Nine of the 13 colonies are represented. They write up a "declaration of rights" and petition the British king and Parliament with them.

November 1765
The Stamp Act goes into effect. It is a day of mourning throughout the colonies. Most businesses are closed, and the colonists almost universally refuse to pay the tax.

March 1766
The Stamp Act is repealed by King George, and the colonial boycott on British imports is lifted after more than a year. Bostonians celebrate on the Boston Common.

June 1767
To prove they are still willing to tax the colonists, Parliament passes the *Townshend Acts* – taxing glass, lead, paint, paper, and tea.

August 1768
In response to the Townshend Acts, merchants in Boston and New York City agree to *boycott British goods* again.

September - October 1768
When riots of protest, and harassment of government officials become big problems in Boston, over 1,000 *British troops* are landed there to help "keep the peace".

May 1769
George Mason & George Washington present *the Virginia Resolves* to the Virginia House of Burgesses, opposing taxation without representation. Virginia agrees to join the boycott of British goods.

March 1770
In Massachusetts, British soldiers open fire to defend themselves, killing five out-of-control civilians. The event is quickly termed "the *Boston Massacre*" by Paul Revere and other radical Americans. British soldiers are then pulled out of Boston, to Castle Island in the Boston Harbor.

April 1770
Parliament cuts back the taxes from the *Townshend Acts* to just the tea tax.

May 1773
Britain's new *Tea Act* reduces the tax on British tea, and basically gives the East India Company merchants a monopoly on selling tea in the colonies. In response to the monopoly, colonists boycott tea.

November 1773
In Massachusetts the tea problem comes to a head when three British ships carrying tea arrive in Boston Harbor. The colonists won't let it unload, and Governor Hutchinson won't let it leave until it's unloaded.

December 1773
Over 100 angry Boston citizens "disguised" as Indians leave to dump the more than 300 cases of tea into the Boston Harbor.
(The Boston Tea Party)

March 1774
The King responds to the Boston Tea Party by passing the *Coercive*, or *Intolerable, Act,* which close the Boston port and put in place stronger *Quartering Acts.* In response, patriots across Massachusetts begin forming "Minute Men" militia units.

May 1774
General Gage replaces Thomas Hutchinson as Massachusetts governor, and puts the colony under *military law.* Four regiments of British troops arrive in Massachusetts soon afterwards.

May 1774
With the growing number of Intolerable Acts, comes the *Quebec Act*, which among other things extends the border of Canada into areas claimed by American colonies.

June 1774
The newest *Quartering Act* once again requires American to house the British troops that have been stationed among them.

July 1774
George Mason and George Washington (both of Fairfax County, Virginia) write *"The Fairfax Resolves"* which protest the British treatment of Americans, call for a general boycott of British goods and support of Boston, and request a meeting of a Continental Congress.

September - October 1774

The First Continental Congress meets in Philadelphia, Pennsylvania with representatives from all of the colonies except Georgia. They agree to boycott British imports, to form committees in each colony to enforce the boycotts, and to start raising local militia units. (One vote/colony.)

March 1775

Patrick Henry gives one of his famous speeches to the Virginia Burgesses, *"…I know not what course others may take, but as for me, give me liberty or give me death."*

March 1775

New England colonists are ordered by Parliament and the King to trade exclusively with Great Britain (the *New England Restraining Act*).

Revolutionary War Begins

April 19, 1775

The first fighting of the war at the Battles of Lexington and Concord: the "shot heard round the world"

May 1775

The Second Continental Congress convenes in Philadelphia, Pennsylvania. John Hancock is elected President of the Congress.

July 1775
Congress petitions King George with the *Olive Branch Petition* (drafted by John Dickinson). It puts the blame on Parliament, rather than on the king, for injuries against the colonies. The king refuses to receive the petition.

July 1775
Continental Congress sends the *Declaration on the Causes and Necessity of Taking Up Arms* to Great Britain. It is written by John Dickinson and Thomas Jefferson.

August 1775
King George declares that all of the colonies have "proceeded to open and avowed rebellion".

December 1775
British Parliament issues the *Prohibitory Act* declaring the colonies to no longer be under the protection of the Crown, ordering a blockade of Colonial ports, and ordering colonial ships to be seized.

January 1776
Thomas Paine's 50-page pamphlet *Common Sense* is published in the American colonies. It criticizes the king, argues for American independence, and is a colonial best-seller almost instantly, selling 500,000 copies (to a population of only 2 million). Paine advocates an immediate declaration of independence, so they can seize the property of loyalists, and be more likely to receive foreign aid.

February 1776
North Carolina patriots win a decisive victory against Scottish loyalists at the Battle of Moore's Creek Bridge.

April 1776
Motivated in part by their recent victory, North Carolina delegates to the Second Continental Congress are instructed to vote for independence (the first delegates so instructed).

May 1776
The Virginia Convention resolves to instruct its delegates in Congress to declare the United Colonies free and independent states.

June 7, 1776
Richard Henry Lee of Virginia presents a resolution to the Continental Congress calling for America's declaration of independence. The resolution sparks much debate in Congress.

June 11, 1776
In response to Lee's resolution, a *committee of five* is formed by Congress to draft the formal declaration of independence.

June 12, 1776
The *Virginia Declaration of Rights*, drafted by George Mason, is adopted by the Virginia Constitutional Convention of Delegates.

June 28, 1776
Thomas Jefferson presents his *draft of the Declaration* (with slight modifications by Benjamin Franklin and John Adams) to the Continental Congress.

June 29, 1776
The Constitution of Virginia, which had been drafted previously by George Mason and Thomas Jefferson, is approved.

July 2, 1776
After much fiery debate, and some delegates showing up just in time, the Continental Congress finally unanimously passes Lee's resolution for independence. (Unanimously meaning each **colony** voted for the resolution – even though some individual **delegates** did not.)

July 4, 1776
After two more days of debating, and some more "minor" changes to Thomas Jefferson's work, the Continental Congress votes unanimously to pass the *Declaration of Independence*.

August 1776
The Declaration of Independence is formally signed by most of the delegates of the Continental Congress; the Continental Congress is now the acting government in the colonies/states.

November 1777
Work on the *Articles of Confederation* (the first constitution of the United States) is long and slow. The biggest fight is how strong the central government should be – delegates do not want to exchange one tyrant for another. It must now be ratified by all 13 states.
(The idea of "E Pluribus Unum" – Out of Many, One" – doesn't catch on until the 2nd Constitution.)

February 1778
The French finally sign a treaty with the Americans, agreeing to aid them in their war against the British.

April 1778
A British Commission is sent to America to offer the colonies "home rule". Congress ratifies the treaty with France, and ignores the offers of the British, since it still does not recognize full independence for the Americans.

March 1781
Americans adopt their first constitution, *The Articles of Confederation*, after it is ratified by all the states. (Maryland is the last to ratify, not wanting to give up its western lands.)

October 19, 1781
Lord Cornwallis surrenders the British army at Yorktown, Virginia to General Washington. The band plays "The world turned upside down." The states have won their war – but now enter into the "Critical Period".

September 1783

The Americans, represented by John Adams, Benjamin Franklin, and others, witness the signing of the peace treaty with England. Benjamin Rush (one of the signers of the Declaration), states: "The American war is over, but the American Revolution is far from over."

War ends, Critical Period begins

All but two states write new constitutions during this time, with most containing a Bill of Rights.

1784

Spain blocks the Mississippi River – endangering trade for the newly formed United States.

1785

U.S. war debt has risen to $10 million (Government can't even keep up with the interest on it). (Continental dollars became worthless.)

With *the Land Ordinance of 1785*, the U.S. announces how it will deal with the western territories.

March 1785
Delegates from Maryland and Virginia meet in Alexandria to discuss commerce, particularly the Potomac River development. After moving the meeting to Mount Vernon, they sign the *Mount Vernon Compact.*[1]

August 1786 – February 1787
Many in Western MA were losing their lands and/or going to jail because they couldn't afford to pay their taxes. They stormed several courthouses to prevent action. Daniel Shays (a former Revolutionary War veteran) - was one of leaders. 600 armed men, mostly farmers, forced the State Supreme Court to close.

The Massachusetts Governor tried to call out the militia, but without a standing arm, it is difficult to put down "Shay's Rebellion". Eventually the governor formed an army with 4,000 mercenaries. The "rebels" were eventually defeated, with just a few deaths.

The difficulty in dealing with Shay's Rebellion leads to calls for a convention to revise the Articles of Confederation.

September 1786
The Annapolis Convention convenes to discuss commerce, and to consider amending the Articles of Confederation – all states are invited, but only five attend (NY, NJ, Penn, Del, VA)

---

[1] George Washington writes John Jay, *"I do not conceive we can exist long as a nation, without having lodged somewhere a power which will pervade the whole Union in as energetic a manner, as the authority of the different state governments extends over the several states."*

1787
Congress passes the *Northwest Ordinance*, legislating how new states will be added to the country, and how they will be governed.

February 1787
Congress approves a second convention to amend the *Articles of Confederation* (this one to be held in Philadelphia[2]).

May 1787
James Madison shows up in Philadelphia with the *Virginia Plan* for making a new constitution. He will keep the best notes throughout the Constitutional Convention.

The Constitutional Convention begins in Philadelphia. All the states except Rhode Island send delegates.
It soon becomes obvious that they wouldn't be able to **fix** the articles, so they scrapped them and started over from scratch.

September 1787
Final draft of Constitution is signed by 39 delegates at the Constitutional Convention. It would need to be ratified by 3/4s of the states (9) to take effect.

---

[2] Philadelphia is a centrally located city which is also the second largest city in North America at the time (second only to Mexico City).

October 1787
First anti-federalist letter is published, trying to convince people not to ratify the new Constitution. The first Federalist paper is published shortly afterwards.

1787 – 1788
James Madison, John Jay, and Alexander Hamilton write the *Federalist Papers*, giving strong arguments in favor of ratifying the Constitution.

June 1788
The new *U.S. Constitution* is ratified by the 9th state, New Hampshire, and becomes "the law of the land".

July 1788
New York ratifies the Constitution.

August 1788
North Carolina rejects the Constitution, since it has no Bill of Rights.

March 1789
The *U.S. Constitution* takes effect.

April 1789
George Washington takes office in New York City as the 1st President of the United States. There are currently 11 states in the Union.

June 1789
As promised, James Madison proposes amendments to the Constitution.

May 1790
Rhode Island, the last of the "original 13 states" finally ratifies the Constitution.

November 1791
The Bill of Rights, the first **10** amendments to U.S. Constitution, is ratified by the states. (It will only be amended 17 more times in over 200 years.)

1863
After his death, James Madison's extensive notes from the Philadelphia (Constitutional) Convention finally become available.

Using Constitution-Related Documents

There are a fair number of documents that I consider critical for background information for understanding the Constitution and its history. Some of them are rather long, so in many cases I've just used excerpts when I cover them with my students. You can see just from the list the long heritage of freedom that the Americans and the British share…

These are the documents I have found the most important in my studying/teaching the U.S. Constitution; you will find the documents or excerpts of the documents, just before the activities at the end of this book.

- Magna Carta (1215)
- The Mayflower Compact (1620)
- Fundamental Orders of Connecticut (1639)
- Massachusetts Body of Liberties (1641)
- English Bill of Rights (1689)
- Resolutions of the Stamp Act (1765)
- Fairfax County (Virginia) Resolves (1774)
- Patrick Henry's "Give Me Liberty or Give Me Death" speech (1775)
- Declaration of the Causes and Necessity of Taking Up Arms (1775)
- Thomas Paine's "Common Sense" pamphlet (1776)
- Virginia Declaration of Rights (1776)
- Constitution of Virginia (1776)
- Declaration of Independence (1776)
- Thomas Paine's "American Crisis" pamphlet (1776)
- Articles of Confederation (ratified between 1777 – 1781)
- Northwest Ordinance (1787)
- Federalist Paper #10 (1787)
- Letters between Danbury Baptists and President Jefferson (1801/1802)

We can see principles that are found in our Constitution in many of these earlier documents of Britain's history, and our history.

It can be helpful to have students find those principles as they go through the different documents. For instance, in the Magna Carta, we see hints of property rights, of juries, etc. In the English Bill of Rights we see many rights that make it into the Virginia Declaration of Rights and then into our Bill of Rights, and so on…

As you follow the trail leading to this great foundational document of our country – on the one hand completely American, and yet on the other, so very British – track these basic freedoms carried from one tradition to another…freedom of religion, of speech, of the press, the right to trial by jury, the prohibition of excessive punishment or double jeopardy, and so much more.

And along the way, pause to consider the economic ramifications of these freedoms – built squarely on the "right to property"…Can any of the others survive without that freedom? (Go through the Constitution with students looking for all of the "economic concepts" there – a lesson appropriate for any government class, economic class, or even American History class…)

What Say the Reeds at Runnymede?

Poem by Rudyard Kipling (1865-1936) about the Signing of the Magna Carta

At Runnymede, at Runnymede,
What say the reeds at Runnymede?
The lissom reeds that give and take,
That bend so far, but never break,
They keep the sleepy Thames awake
With tales of John at Runnymede.

        At Runnymede, at Runnymede,
        Oh, hear the reeds at Runnymede:
        'You musn't sell, delay, deny,
        A freeman's right or liberty.
        It wakes the stubborn Englishry,
        We saw 'em roused at Runnymede!

When through our ranks the Barons came,
With little thought of praise or blame,
But resolute to play the game,
They lumbered up to Runnymede;
And there they launched in solid line
The first attack on Right Divine,
The curt uncompromising "Sign!"
They settled John at Runnymede.

        At Runnymede, at Runnymede,
        Your rights were won at Runnymede!
        No freeman shall be fined or bound,
        Or dispossessed of freehold ground,
        Except by lawful judgment found
        And passed upon him by his peers.
        Forget not, after all these years,
        The Charter signed at Runnymede.

And still when mob or Monarch lays
Too rude a hand on English ways,
The whisper wakes, the shudder plays,
Across the reeds at Runnymede.
And Thames, that knows the moods of kings,
And crowds and priests and suchlike things,
Rolls deep and dreadful as he brings
Their warning down from Runnymede!

The U.S. Constitution: Articles

The Constitution has 7 articles:

Article 1.   Legislative Branch   makes law
                (House, Senate)

Article 2.   Executive Branch   enforces law
                (President, Vice President, Attorney General)

Article 3.   Judicial Branch   interprets law
                (Supreme Court, Federal Courts)

Article 4.   Concerning the States
                -- Records of each state to be recognized by each other
                -- Extradition (legal way to move criminals to other state)

Article 5.   How to Amend the Constitution
                -- 2/3s of states to propose amendment
                -- 3/4s of states to amend

Article 6.   Supreme Law of Land = the U.S. Constitution
                -- State constitutions cannot go against it

Article 7.   Ratification requires 3/4s of the states

The Constitution of the United States

We the People of the United States, in Order to form a more perfect Union, establish Justice, insure domestic Tranquility, provide for the common defence, promote the general Welfare, and secure the Blessings of Liberty to ourselves and our Posterity, do ordain and establish this Constitution for the United States of America.

Article. I.

Section. 1. All legislative Powers herein granted shall be vested in a Congress of the United States, which shall consist of a Senate and House of Representatives.

Section. 2. The House of Representatives shall be composed of Members chosen every second Year by the People of the several States, and the Electors in each State shall have the Qualifications requisite for Electors of the most numerous Branch of the State Legislature.

No Person shall be a Representative who shall not have attained to the Age of twenty five Years, and been seven Years a Citizen of the United States, and who shall not, when elected, be an Inhabitant of that State in which he shall be chosen.

Representatives and direct Taxes shall be apportioned among the several States which may be included within this Union, according to their respective Numbers, which shall be determined by adding to the whole Number of free Persons, including those bound to Service for a Term of Years, and excluding Indians not taxed, three fifths of all other Persons. The actual Enumeration shall be made within three Years after the first Meeting of the Congress of the United States, and within every subsequent Term of ten Years, in such Manner as they shall by Law direct. The Number of Representatives shall not exceed one for every thirty Thousand, but each State shall have at Least one Representative; and until such enumeration shall be made, the State of New Hampshire shall be entitled to chuse three, Massachusetts eight, Rhode-Island and Providence Plantations one, Connecticut five, New-York six, New Jersey four, Pennsylvania eight, Delaware one, Maryland six, Virginia ten, North Carolina five, South Carolina five, and Georgia three.

When vacancies happen in the Representation from any State, the Executive Authority thereof shall issue Writs of Election to fill such Vacancies.

The House of Representatives shall chuse their Speaker and other Officers; and shall have the sole Power of Impeachment.

Section. 3. The Senate of the United States shall be composed of two Senators from each State, chosen by the Legislature thereof for six Years; and each Senator shall have one Vote.

Immediately after they shall be assembled in Consequence of the first Election, they shall be divided as equally as may be into three Classes. The Seats of the Senators of the first Class shall be vacated at the Expiration of the second Year, of the second Class at the Expiration of the fourth Year, and of the third Class at the Expiration of the sixth Year, so that one third may be chosen every second Year; and if Vacancies happen by Resignation, or otherwise, during the Recess of the Legislature of any State, the Executive thereof may make temporary Appointments until the next Meeting of the Legislature, which shall then fill such Vacancies.

No Person shall be a Senator who shall not have attained to the Age of thirty Years, and been nine Years a Citizen of the United States, and who shall not, when elected, be an Inhabitant of that State for which he shall be chosen.

The Vice President of the United States shall be President of the Senate, but shall have no Vote, unless they be equally divided.

The Senate shall chuse their other Officers, and also a President pro tempore, in the Absence of the Vice President, or when he shall exercise the Office of President of the United States.

The Senate shall have the sole Power to try all Impeachments. When sitting for that Purpose, they shall be on Oath or Affirmation. When the President of the United States is tried, the Chief Justice shall preside: And no Person shall be convicted without the Concurrence of two thirds of the Members present.

Judgment in Cases of Impeachment shall not extend further than to removal from Office, and disqualification to hold and enjoy any Office of honor, Trust or Profit under the United States: but the Party convicted shall nevertheless be liable and subject to Indictment, Trial, Judgment and Punishment, according to Law.

Section. 4. The Times, Places and Manner of holding Elections for Senators and Representatives, shall be prescribed in each State by the Legislature thereof; but the Congress may at any time by Law make or alter such Regulations, except as to the Places of chusing Senators.

The Congress shall assemble at least once in every Year, and such Meeting shall be on the first Monday in December, unless they shall by Law appoint a different Day.

Section. 5. Each House shall be the Judge of the Elections, Returns and Qualifications of its own Members, and a Majority of each shall constitute a Quorum to do Business; but a smaller Number may adjourn from day to day, and may be authorized to compel the Attendance of absent Members, in such Manner, and under such Penalties as each House may provide.

Each House may determine the Rules of its Proceedings, punish its Members for disorderly Behaviour, and, with the Concurrence of two thirds, expel a Member.

Each House shall keep a Journal of its Proceedings, and from time to time publish the same, excepting such Parts as may in their Judgment require Secrecy; and the Yeas and Nays of the Members of either House on any question shall, at the Desire of one fifth of those Present, be entered on the Journal.

Neither House, during the Session of Congress, shall, without the Consent of the other, adjourn for more than three days, nor to any other Place than that in which the two Houses shall be sitting.

Section. 6. The Senators and Representatives shall receive a Compensation for their Services, to be ascertained by Law, and paid out of the Treasury of the United States. They shall in all Cases, except Treason, Felony and Breach of the Peace, be privileged from Arrest during their Attendance at the Session of their respective Houses, and in going to and returning from the same; and for any Speech or Debate in either House, they shall not be questioned in any other Place.

No Senator or Representative shall, during the Time for which he was elected, be appointed to any civil Office under the Authority of the United States, which shall have been created, or the Emoluments whereof shall have been encreased during such time; and no Person holding any Office under the United States, shall be a Member of either House during his Continuance in Office.

Section. 7. All Bills for raising Revenue shall originate in the House of Representatives; but the Senate may propose or concur with Amendments as on other Bills.

Every Bill which shall have passed the House of Representatives and the Senate, shall, before it become a Law, be presented to the President of the United States: If he approve he shall sign it, but if not he shall return it, with his Objections to that House in which it shall have originated, who shall enter the Objections at large on their Journal, and proceed to reconsider it. If after such Reconsideration two thirds of that House shall agree to pass the Bill, it shall be sent, together with the Objections, to the other House, by which it shall likewise be reconsidered, and if approved by two thirds of that House, it shall become a Law. But in all such Cases the Votes of both Houses shall be determined by yeas and Nays, and the Names of the Persons voting for and against the Bill shall be entered on the Journal of each House respectively. If any Bill shall not be returned by the President within ten Days (Sundays excepted) after it shall have been presented to him, the Same shall be a Law, in like Manner as if he had signed it, unless the Congress by their Adjournment prevent its Return, in which Case it shall not be a Law.

Every Order, Resolution, or Vote to which the Concurrence of the Senate and House of Representatives may be necessary (except on a question of Adjournment) shall be presented to the President of the United States; and before the Same shall take Effect, shall be approved by him, or being disapproved by him, shall be repassed by two thirds of the Senate and House of Representatives, according to the Rules and Limitations prescribed in the Case of a Bill.

Section. 8. The Congress shall have Power To lay and collect Taxes, Duties, Imposts and Excises, to pay the Debts and provide for the common Defence and general Welfare of the United States; but all Duties, Imposts and Excises shall be uniform throughout the United States;

> To borrow Money on the credit of the United States;

> To regulate Commerce with foreign Nations, and among the several States, and with the Indian Tribes;

> To establish an uniform Rule of Naturalization, and uniform Laws on the subject of Bankruptcies throughout the United States;

> To coin Money, regulate the Value thereof, and of foreign Coin, and fix the Standard of Weights and Measures;

> To provide for the Punishment of counterfeiting the Securities and current Coin of the United States;

> To establish Post Offices and post Roads;

> To promote the Progress of Science and useful Arts, by securing for limited Times to Authors and Inventors the exclusive Right to their respective Writings and Discoveries;

> To constitute Tribunals inferior to the supreme Court;

> To define and punish Piracies and Felonies committed on the high Seas, and Offences against the Law of Nations;

To declare War, grant Letters of Marque and Reprisal, and make Rules concerning Captures on Land and Water;

To raise and support Armies, but no Appropriation of Money to that Use shall be for a longer Term than two Years;

To provide and maintain a Navy;

To make Rules for the Government and Regulation of the land and naval Forces;

To provide for calling forth the Militia to execute the Laws of the Union, suppress Insurrections and repel Invasions;

To provide for organizing, arming, and disciplining, the Militia, and for governing such Part of them as may be employed in the Service of the United States, reserving to the States respectively, the Appointment of the Officers, and the Authority of training the Militia according to the discipline prescribed by Congress;

To exercise exclusive Legislation in all Cases whatsoever, over such District (not exceeding ten Miles square) as may, by Cession of particular States, and the Acceptance of Congress, become the Seat of the Government of the United States, and to exercise like Authority over all Places purchased by the Consent of the Legislature of the State in which the Same shall be, for the Erection of Forts, Magazines, Arsenals, dock-Yards, and other needful Buildings;--And

To make all Laws which shall be necessary and proper for carrying into Execution the foregoing Powers, and all other Powers vested by this Constitution in the Government of the United States, or in any Department or Officer thereof.

Section. 9. The Migration or Importation of such Persons as any of the States now existing shall think proper to admit, shall not be prohibited by the Congress prior to the Year one thousand eight hundred and eight, but a Tax or duty may be imposed on such Importation, not exceeding ten dollars for each Person.

The Privilege of the Writ of Habeas Corpus shall not be suspended, unless when in Cases of Rebellion or Invasion the public Safety may require it.

No Bill of Attainder or ex post facto Law shall be passed.

No Capitation, or other direct, Tax shall be laid, unless in Proportion to the Census or enumeration herein before directed to be taken.

No Tax or Duty shall be laid on Articles exported from any State.

No Preference shall be given by any Regulation of Commerce or Revenue to the Ports of one State over those of another; nor shall Vessels bound to, or from, one State, be obliged to enter, clear, or pay Duties in another.

No Money shall be drawn from the Treasury, but in Consequence of Appropriations made by Law; and a regular Statement and Account of the Receipts and Expenditures of all public Money shall be published from time to time.

No Title of Nobility shall be granted by the United States: And no Person holding any Office of Profit or Trust under them, shall, without the Consent of the Congress, accept of any present, Emolument, Office, or Title, of any kind whatever, from any King, Prince, or foreign State.

Section. 10. No State shall enter into any Treaty, Alliance, or Confederation; grant Letters of Marque and Reprisal; coin Money; emit Bills of Credit; make any Thing but gold and silver Coin a Tender in Payment of Debts; pass any Bill of Attainder, ex post facto Law, or Law impairing the Obligation of Contracts, or grant any Title of Nobility.

No State shall, without the Consent of the Congress, lay any Imposts or Duties on Imports or Exports, except what may be absolutely necessary for executing it's inspection Laws: and the net Produce of all Duties and Imposts, laid by any State on Imports or Exports, shall be for the Use of the Treasury of the United States; and all such Laws shall be subject to the Revision and Controul of the Congress.

No State shall, without the Consent of Congress, lay any Duty of Tonnage, keep Troops, or Ships of War in time of Peace, enter into any Agreement or Compact with another State, or with a foreign Power, or engage in War, unless actually invaded, or in such imminent Danger as will not admit of delay.

Article. II.

Section. 1. The executive Power shall be vested in a President of the United States of America. He shall hold his Office during the Term of four Years, and, together with the Vice President, chosen for the same Term, be elected, as follows:

Each State shall appoint, in such Manner as the Legislature thereof may direct, a Number of Electors, equal to the whole Number of Senators and Representatives to which the State may be entitled in the Congress: but no Senator or Representative, or Person holding an Office of Trust or Profit under the United States, shall be appointed an Elector.

The Electors shall meet in their respective States, and vote by Ballot for two Persons, of whom one at least shall not be an Inhabitant of the same State with themselves. And they shall make a List of all the Persons voted for, and of the Number of Votes for each; which List they shall sign and certify, and transmit sealed to the Seat of the Government of the United States, directed to the President of the Senate. The President of the Senate shall, in the Presence of the Senate and House of Representatives, open all the Certificates, and the Votes shall then be counted. The Person having the greatest Number of Votes shall be the President, if such Number be a Majority of the whole Number of Electors appointed; and if there be more than one who have such Majority, and have an equal Number of Votes, then the House of Representatives shall immediately chuse by Ballot one of them for President; and if no Person have a Majority, then from the five highest on the List the said House shall in like Manner chuse the President. But in chusing the President, the Votes shall be taken by States, the Representation from each State having one Vote; A quorum for this purpose shall consist of a

Member or Members from two thirds of the States, and a Majority of all the States shall be necessary to a Choice. In every Case, after the Choice of the President, the Person having the greatest Number of Votes of the Electors shall be the Vice President. But if there should remain two or more who have equal Votes, the Senate shall chuse from them by Ballot the Vice President.

The Congress may determine the Time of chusing the Electors, and the Day on which they shall give their Votes; which Day shall be the same throughout the United States.

No Person except a natural born Citizen, or a Citizen of the United States, at the time of the Adoption of this Constitution, shall be eligible to the Office of President; neither shall any Person be eligible to that Office who shall not have attained to the Age of thirty five Years, and been fourteen Years a Resident within the United States.

In Case of the Removal of the President from Office, or of his Death, Resignation, or Inability to discharge the Powers and Duties of the said Office, the Same shall devolve on the Vice President, and the Congress may by Law provide for the Case of Removal, Death, Resignation or Inability, both of the President and Vice President, declaring what Officer shall then act as President, and such Officer shall act accordingly, until the Disability be removed, or a President shall be elected.

The President shall, at stated Times, receive for his Services, a Compensation, which shall neither be increased nor diminished during the Period for which he shall have been elected, and he shall not receive within that Period any other Emolument from the United States, or any of them.

Before he enter on the Execution of his Office, he shall take the following Oath or Affirmation:--"I do solemnly swear (or affirm) that I will faithfully execute the Office of President of the United States, and will to the best of my Ability, preserve, protect and defend the Constitution of the United States."

Section. 2. The President shall be Commander in Chief of the Army and Navy of the United States, and of the Militia of the several States, when called into the actual Service of the United States; he may require the Opinion, in writing, of the principal Officer in each of the executive Departments, upon any Subject relating to the Duties of their respective Offices, and he shall have Power to grant Reprieves and Pardons for Offences against the United States, except in Cases of Impeachment.

He shall have Power, by and with the Advice and Consent of the Senate, to make Treaties, provided two thirds of the Senators present concur; and he shall nominate, and by and with the Advice and Consent of the Senate, shall appoint Ambassadors, other public Ministers and Consuls, Judges of the supreme Court, and all other Officers of the United States, whose Appointments are not herein otherwise provided for, and which shall be established by Law: but the Congress may by Law vest the Appointment of such inferior Officers, as they think proper, in the President alone, in the Courts of Law, or in the Heads of Departments.

The President shall have Power to fill up all Vacancies that may happen during the Recess of the Senate, by granting Commissions which shall expire at the End of their next Session.

Section. 3. He shall from time to time give to the Congress Information of the State of the Union, and recommend to their

Consideration such Measures as he shall judge necessary and expedient; he may, on extraordinary Occasions, convene both Houses, or either of them, and in Case of Disagreement between them, with Respect to the Time of Adjournment, he may adjourn them to such Time as he shall think proper; he shall receive Ambassadors and other public Ministers; he shall take Care that the Laws be faithfully executed, and shall Commission all the Officers of the United States.

Section. 4. The President, Vice President and all civil Officers of the United States, shall be removed from Office on Impeachment for, and Conviction of, Treason, Bribery, or other high Crimes and Misdemeanors.

Article III.

Section. 1. The judicial Power of the United States shall be vested in one supreme Court, and in such inferior Courts as the Congress may from time to time ordain and establish. The Judges, both of the supreme and inferior Courts, shall hold their Offices during good Behaviour, and shall, at stated Times, receive for their Services a Compensation, which shall not be diminished during their Continuance in Office.

Section. 2. The judicial Power shall extend to all Cases, in Law and Equity, arising under this Constitution, the Laws of the United States, and Treaties made, or which shall be made, under their Authority;--to all Cases affecting Ambassadors, other public Ministers and Consuls;--to all Cases of admiralty and maritime Jurisdiction;--to Controversies to which the United States shall be a Party;--to Controversies between two or more States;--between a State and Citizens of another State,--between Citizens of different States,--between Citizens of the same State claiming Lands under Grants of different States, and between a State, or the Citizens thereof, and foreign States, Citizens or Subjects.

In all Cases affecting Ambassadors, other public Ministers and Consuls, and those in which a State shall be Party, the supreme Court shall have original Jurisdiction. In all the other Cases before mentioned, the supreme Court shall have appellate Jurisdiction, both as to Law and Fact, with such Exceptions, and under such Regulations as the Congress shall make.

The Trial of all Crimes, except in Cases of Impeachment, shall be by Jury; and such Trial shall be held in the State where the said Crimes shall have been committed; but when not committed within any

State, the Trial shall be at such Place or Places as the Congress may by Law have directed.

Section. 3. Treason against the United States, shall consist only in levying War against them, or in adhering to their Enemies, giving them Aid and Comfort. No Person shall be convicted of Treason unless on the Testimony of two Witnesses to the same overt Act, or on Confession in open Court.

The Congress shall have Power to declare the Punishment of Treason, but no Attainder of Treason shall work Corruption of Blood, or Forfeiture except during the Life of the Person attainted.

Article. IV.

Section. 1. Full Faith and Credit shall be given in each State to the public Acts, Records, and judicial Proceedings of every other State. And the Congress may by general Laws prescribe the Manner in which such Acts, Records and Proceedings shall be proved, and the Effect thereof.

Section. 2. The Citizens of each State shall be entitled to all Privileges and Immunities of Citizens in the several States.

A Person charged in any State with Treason, Felony, or other Crime, who shall flee from Justice, and be found in another State, shall on Demand of the executive Authority of the State from which he fled, be delivered up, to be removed to the State having Jurisdiction of the Crime.

No Person held to Service or Labour in one State, under the Laws thereof, escaping into another, shall, in Consequence of any Law or Regulation therein, be discharged from such Service or Labour, but shall be delivered up on Claim of the Party to whom such Service or Labour may be due.

Section. 3. New States may be admitted by the Congress into this Union; but no new State shall be formed or erected within the Jurisdiction of any other State; nor any State be formed by the Junction of two or more States, or Parts of States, without the Consent of the Legislatures of the States concerned as well as of the Congress.

The Congress shall have Power to dispose of and make all needful Rules and Regulations respecting the Territory or other Property belonging to the United States; and nothing in this Constitution shall be so construed as to Prejudice any Claims of the United States, or of any particular State.

Section. 4. The United States shall guarantee to every State in this Union a Republican Form of Government, and shall protect each of them against Invasion; and on Application of the Legislature, or of the Executive (when the Legislature cannot be convened), against domestic Violence.

Article. V.

The Congress, whenever two thirds of both Houses shall deem it necessary, shall propose Amendments to this Constitution, or, on the Application of the Legislatures of two thirds of the several States, shall call a Convention for proposing Amendments, which, in either Case, shall be valid to all Intents and Purposes, as Part of this Constitution, when ratified by the Legislatures of three fourths of the several States, or by Conventions in three fourths thereof, as the one or the other Mode of Ratification may be proposed by the Congress; Provided that no Amendment which may be made prior to the Year One thousand eight hundred and eight shall in any Manner affect the first and fourth Clauses in the Ninth Section of the first Article; and that no State, without its Consent, shall be deprived of its equal Suffrage in the Senate.

Article. VI.

All Debts contracted and Engagements entered into, before the Adoption of this Constitution, shall be as valid against the United States under this Constitution, as under the Confederation.

This Constitution, and the Laws of the United States which shall be made in Pursuance thereof; and all Treaties made, or which shall be made, under the Authority of the United States, shall be the supreme Law of the Land; and the Judges in every State shall be bound thereby, any Thing in the Constitution or Laws of any State to the Contrary notwithstanding.

The Senators and Representatives before mentioned, and the Members of the several State Legislatures, and all executive and judicial Officers, both of the United States and of the several States, shall be bound by Oath or Affirmation, to support this Constitution; but no religious Test shall ever be required as a Qualification to any Office or public Trust under the United States.

Article. VII.

The Ratification of the Conventions of nine States, shall be sufficient for the Establishment of this Constitution between the States so ratifying the Same.

The Word, "the," being interlined between the seventh and eighth Lines of the first Page, the Word "Thirty" being partly written on an Erazure in the fifteenth Line of the first Page, The Words "is tried" being interlined between the thirty second and thirty third Lines of the first Page and the Word "the" being interlined between the forty third and forty fourth Lines of the second Page.

Attest William Jackson Secretary

Done in Convention by the Unanimous Consent of the States present the Seventeenth Day of September in the Year of our Lord one thousand seven hundred and Eighty seven and of the Independence of the United States of America the Twelfth In witness whereof We have hereunto subscribed our Names,

G°. Washington
Presidt and deputy from Virginia

Bill of Rights (1st 10 amendments)
With Explanations

1st Amendment: *Congress shall make no law respecting an establishment of religion, or prohibiting the free exercise thereof; or abridging the freedom of speech, or of the press; or the right of the people peaceably to assemble, and to petition the Government for a redress of grievances.*

= "religious constraints on the government, and the people's freedom of speech, the press, the right to peaceably assemble, and to petition the government"

Prior to the first amendment, the only one reference to religion in the Constitution was prohibiting religious tests for public office in the federal government.

Until a ruling by the Supreme Court in th 1920's, the 1st Amendment was only seen as a deterrent to the Federal Government, not to the state governments.

Religious Constraints
1st part of 1st amendment:
"Congress shall make no law respecting an establishment of religion"

Various interpretations of this portion of the amendment:
<u>Broad interpretation</u> – no government support for religion at all
- Government cannot establish a church
- Cannot support any religious activities…
- Cannot give aid or support – even if to ALL religions
- ("In God we Trust" and "under God" in the pledge not allowed)

- Cannot put up religious displays at all

Narrow interpretation – government only prohibited from partial treatment
- Cannot establish a church
- Can support all religions
- Can put "In God we trust" on money
- Cannot put one type of religious displays – unless does others

Literal interpretation – only prohibits **national** religion
- Can put up limited religious displays

2nd part of Religious portion of 1st amendment:
"Congress…shall make no law…prohibiting the free exercise (of religion)…

Supreme Court has ruled we may BELIEVE anything we want; but PRACTICE has limitations.

One consideration – "Does government have a compelling interest?"
Other consideration – "Does it break important and fair laws?"
- Religious practices involving polygamy and illegal drugs – are generally not allowed

Freedom of Speech
Next parts of 1st amendment:
"Congress…shall make no law…abridging the freedom of speech…"

But, freedom of speech **is** limited by time, place, and manner…
- Obscenity has not been protected (typically)

- "Clear and present danger" speech not allowed
- Lying under oath
- Nor national security secrets
- Nor Libel
- Nor speech that leads to a riot, or causes violence…

Freedom of the Press
"Congress…shall make no law…abridging the freedom of … the press…"

Thomas Jefferson wrote from France, "Were it left to me to decide whether we should have a government without newspapers or newspapers without a government, I should not hesitate for a moment to prefer the latter."

Examples of abridging the freedom of the press:
- Trial of John Peter Zenger (printer accused of libel) in 1735
- Sedition Act of 1798
- Prior to the Civil War – some states had laws outlawing abolitionist material…
- After President McKinley's assassination by an anarchist in 1901, some states passed laws forbidding the advocating of the overthrow of the government by force…
- 1918 Espionage Act – prohibiting resistance to the U.S. war effort
- After World War I – some states passed peacetime sedition laws

Question to consider/discuss: What about during war time – should there be any limits on the press then?

Freedom to Assemble Peaceably:
"Congress…shall make no law…abridging the … right of the people peaceably to assemble, and to petition the Government for a redress of grievances."

The freedom to assemble and right of petition go back to the Magna Carta, are currently listed in almost all state constitutions.

The freedom to assemble has been revoked:
- 1894--when homeless/unemployed marched on Washington and President Cleveland had them arrested
- Great Depression—World War I vets marched on Washington for their military bonus – President Hoover had them fired upon by the U.S. Army
- Allowed in the '60's (sometimes) – during Civil Rights marches

"Freedom of assembly"
    Is also limited by time, place and manner

Public places are generally acceptable – parks, streets, etc…

(The Courts also assume freedom of association is implied by "freedom of assembly" and rule accordingly.)

2nd Amendment: *A well regulated Militia, being necessary to the security of a free State, the right of the people to keep and bear Arms, shall not be infringed.*

Federalist Paper #46 deals with the 2nd amendment.
2nd amendment limited to Congress not infringing (didn't extend to states w/ 14th amendment?)

Only a couple of Supreme Court cases have dealt with the 2nd amendment: *U.S. v. Cruikshank* (1876), *Presser v. Illinois* (1886), *Miller v. Texas* (1894), *U.S. v. Miller* (1939), and *Lewis v. U.S.* (1980)

In the recent case (2008) *District of Columbia Et al. v. Heller* the Supreme Court found in part: "The Second Amendment protects an individual right to possess a firearm unconnected with service in a militia, and to use that arm for traditionally lawful purposes, such as self-defense within the home."

The Supreme Court has generally refused to incorporate (apply to the states) the 2nd amendment.

3rd Amendment: *No Soldier shall, in time of peace be quartered in any house, without the consent of the Owner, nor in time of war, but in a manner to be prescribed by law.*

= "prohibition against quartering troops"

Not a problem in our days, but was a problem before and during the Revolutionary War, just prior to when the Constitution was being written. The British were making a habit of housing their soldiers in the homes of Bostonians during the time of "The Intolerable Acts".

4th Amendment: *The right of the people to be secure in their persons, houses, papers, and effects, against unreasonable searches and seizures, shall not be violated, and no Warrants shall issue, but upon probable cause, supported by Oath or affirmation, and particularly describing the place to be searched, and the persons or things to be seized.*

="prohibition against unreasonable searches and seizures"

Again, a major problem before and during the Revolutionary War; the British were using "writs of assistance" to search homes of colonists without cause. The Constitution brought an end to these government abuses.

The Supreme Court has ruled evidence as inadmissible if it was found in an illegal search.

5th Amendment: *No person shall be held to answer for a capital, or otherwise infamous crime, unless on a presentment or indictment of a Grand Jury, except in cases arising in the land or naval forces, or in the Militia, when in actual service in time of War or public danger; nor shall any person be subject for the same offence to be twice put in jeopardy of life or limb; nor shall be compelled in any criminal case to be a witness against himself, nor be deprived of life, liberty, or property, without due process of law; nor shall private property be taken for public use, without just compensation.*

= "rights of the accused – right to Grand Jury indictment and protection against double jeopardy, testifying against oneself, and loss of life, liberty, or property without due process of law"

Most people know (or think they know) the 5th amendment. It is mentioned frequently, like the 1st amendment, though it's doubtful that most of those who are "pleading the fifth" fully appreciate its full meaning.

This amendment gives us many of our rights in regards to arrest and trial: right to a formal accusation by a Grand Jury, in the case of a serious crime; can't be tried twice for the same crime; don't have to testify against oneself in a trial; cannot be denied life, liberty, or property without "due process of law"; cannot have our property taken by the government without being adequately reimbursed for it.

This is where "Miranda rights" come from: the Supreme Court in 1966 in *Miranda v. Arizona*, determined that police must inform those that have been arrested of their rights to remain silent and not to have to speak out against themselves.

6ᵗʰ Amendment: *In all criminal prosecutions, the accused shall enjoy the right to a speedy and public trial, by an impartial jury of the State and district wherein the crime shall have been committed, which district shall have been previously ascertained by law, and to be informed of the nature and cause of the accusation; to be confronted with the witnesses against him; to have compulsory process for obtaining witnesses in his favor, and to have the Assistance of Counsel for his defense.*

= "right to speedy and fair trial by jury; and right to face witnesses; and right to have defense lawyer"

This is the amendment that guarantees us each fair treatment in the case of an arrest, and subsequent trial. The founding fathers clearly set out the necessary parts of a fair trial on the federal level, and after the 14ᵗʰ amendment, the Supreme Court extended these same guarantees to trials at the state level.

7ᵗʰ Amendment: *In suits at common law, where the value in controversy shall exceed twenty dollars, the right of trial by jury shall be preserved, and no fact tried by a jury, shall be otherwise reexamined in any Court of the United States, than according to the rules of the common law.*

= "right to trial by jury in civil trials"

8th Amendment: *Excessive bail shall not be required, nor excessive fines imposed, nor cruel and unusual punishments inflicted.*

= "unreasonable bail or punishment prohibited"

9th Amendment: *The enumeration in the Constitution, of certain rights, shall not be construed to deny or disparage others retained by the people.*

= "rights not specified are still retained by the people"

10th Amendment: *The powers not delegated to the United States by the Constitution, nor prohibited by it to the States, are reserved to the States respectively, or to the people.*

= "powers not given the federal government specifically are retained by the states and the people"

The 10th Amendment has become increasingly more popular, as people look at what the National Government is doing lately.

Rest of amendments

11ᵗʰ Amendment (1795): *The Judicial power of the United States shall not be construed to extend to any suit in law or equity, commenced or prosecuted against one of the United States by Citizens of another State, or by Citizens or Subjects of any Foreign State.*

= Citizen from one state (or country) cannot sue another state

12th Amendment (1804): *The Electors shall meet in their respective states and vote by ballot for President and Vice-President, one of whom, at least, shall not be an inhabitant of the same state with themselves; they shall name in their ballots the person voted for as President, and in distinct ballots the person voted for as Vice-President, and they shall make distinct lists of all persons voted for as President, and of all persons voted for as Vice-President, and of the number of votes for each, which lists they shall sign and certify, and transmit sealed to the seat of the government of the United States, directed to the President of the Senate; -- the President of the Senate shall, in the presence of the Senate and House of Representatives, open all the certificates and the votes shall then be counted; -- The person having the greatest number of votes for President, shall be the President, if such number be a majority of the whole number of Electors appointed; and if no person have such majority, then from the persons having the highest numbers not exceeding three on the list of those voted for as President, the House of Representatives shall choose immediately, by ballot, the President. But in choosing the President, the votes shall be taken by states, the representation from each state having one vote; a quorum for this purpose shall consist of a member or members from two-thirds of the states, and a majority of all the states shall be necessary to a choice. And if the House of Representatives shall not choose a President whenever the right of choice shall devolve upon them, before the fourth day of March next following, then the Vice-President shall act as President, as in case of the death or other constitutional disability of the President. -- The person having the greatest number of votes as Vice-President, shall be the Vice-President, if such number be a majority of the whole number of Electors appointed, and if no person have a majority, then from the two highest numbers on the list, the Senate shall choose the Vice-President; a quorum for the purpose shall consist of two-thirds of the whole number of Senators, and a majority of the whole number shall be necessary to a choice. But no person constitutionally ineligible to the office of President shall be eligible to that of Vice-President of the United States.*

= Fixed way we elect president and vice-president

More than 60 years passed before the next amendments were made.

13th Amendment (1865): *Section 1.* *Neither slavery nor involuntary servitude, except as a punishment for crime whereof the party shall have been duly convicted, shall exist within the United States, or any place subject to their jurisdiction.* *Section 2.* *Congress shall have power to enforce this article by appropriate legislation.*

= Abolition of slavery

14th Amendment (1866): *Section 1. All persons born or naturalized in the United States, and subject to the jurisdiction thereof, are citizens of the United States and of the State wherein they reside. No State shall make or enforce any law which shall abridge the privileges or immunities of citizens of the United States; nor shall any State deprive any person of life, liberty, or property, without due process of law; nor deny to any person within its jurisdiction the equal protection of the laws. **Section 2.** Representatives shall be apportioned among the several States according to their respective numbers, counting the whole number of persons in each State, excluding Indians not taxed. But when the right to vote at any election for the choice of electors for President and Vice-President of the United States, Representatives in Congress, the Executive and Judicial officers of a State, or the members of the Legislature thereof, is denied to any of the male inhabitants of such State, being twenty-one years of age, and citizens of the United States, or in any way abridged, except for participation in rebellion, or other crime, the basis of representation therein shall be reduced in the proportion which the number of such male citizens shall bear to the whole number of male citizens twenty-one years of age in such State. **Section 3.** No person shall be a Senator or Representative in Congress, or elector of President and Vice-President, or hold any office, civil or military, under the United States, or under any State, who, having previously taken an oath, as a member of Congress, or as an officer of the United States, or as a member of any State legislature, or as an executive or judicial officer of any State, to support the Constitution of the United States, shall have engaged in insurrection or rebellion against the same, or given aid or comfort to the enemies thereof. But Congress may by a vote of two-thirds of each House, remove such disability. **Section 4.** The validity of the public debt of the United States, authorized by law, including debts incurred for payment of pensions and bounties for services in suppressing insurrection or rebellion, shall not be questioned. But neither the United States nor any State shall assume or pay any debt or obligation incurred in aid of insurrection or rebellion against the United States, or any claim for the loss or emancipation of any slave; but all such debts, obligations and claims shall be held illegal and void. **Section 5.** The Congress shall have the power to enforce, by appropriate legislation, the provisions of this article.*

= **Section 1** – definition of a citizen; states cannot take away rights of citizens; Section 2 – number of representatives apportioned…; all male citizens 21 year old and older; **Section 3** – former U.S. legislators and officers who took an oath for the confederacy cannot now serve again as U.S. officers or legislator (removed in 1898).

(In the 1920's the Supreme Court used the 14th Amendment to incorporate (apply) most of the rights in the Bill of Rights to the states.)

15th Amendment (1870): ***Section 1.*** *The right of citizens of the United States to vote shall not be denied or abridged by the United States or by any State on account of race, color, or previous condition of servitude-* ***Section 2.*** *The Congress shall have the power to enforce this article by appropriate legislation.*

= Gave blacks the right to vote – any person or any color

Another 40 years would pass before the Constitution would be amended again.

16th Amendment (1913): *The Congress shall have power to lay and collect taxes on incomes, from whatever source derived, without apportionment among the several States, and without regard to any census or enumeration.*

= Congress empowered to collect Income taxes

17th Amendment (1913) *The Senate of the United States shall be composed of two Senators from each State, elected by the people thereof, for six years; and each Senator shall have one vote. The electors in each State shall have the qualifications requisite for electors of the most numerous branch of the State legislatures.*

When vacancies happen in the representation of any State in the Senate, the executive authority of such State shall issue writs of election to fill such vacancies: Provided, That the legislature of any State may empower the executive thereof to make temporary appointments until the people fill the vacancies by election as the legislature may direct.

This amendment shall not be so construed as to affect the election or term of any Senator chosen before it becomes valid as part of the Constitution.

= Senators will now be elected by the people, rather than by the state legislatures

18th Amendment (1919) **Section 1.** *After one year from the ratification of this article the manufacture, sale, or transportation of intoxicating liquors within, the importation thereof into, or the exportation thereof from the United States and all territory subject to the jurisdiction thereof for beverage purposes is hereby prohibited.* **Section 2.** *The Congress and the several States shall have concurrent power to enforce this article by appropriate legislation.* **Section 3.** *This article shall be inoperative unless it shall have been ratified as an amendment to the Constitution by the legislatures of the several States, as provided in the Constitution, within seven years from the date of the submission hereof to the States by the Congress.*

= Prohibition of alcoholic beverages

19th Amendment (1920) *The right of citizens of the United States to vote shall not be denied or abridged by the United States or by any State on account of sex. Congress shall have power to enforce this article by appropriate legislation.*

= Women given the right to vote in ALL states (15 states had already granted it)

20th Amendment (1933) *Section 1. The terms of the President and the Vice President shall end at noon on the 20th day of January, and the terms of Senators and Representatives at noon on the 3d day of January, of the years in which such terms would have ended if this article had not been ratified; and the terms of their successors shall then begin. Section 2. The Congress shall assemble at least once in every year, and such meeting shall begin at noon on the 3d day of January, unless they shall by law appoint a different day. Section 3. If, at the time fixed for the beginning of the term of the President, the President elect shall have died, the Vice President elect shall become President. If a President shall not have been chosen before the time fixed for the beginning of his term, or if the President elect shall have failed to qualify, then the Vice President elect shall act as President until a President shall have qualified; and the Congress may by law provide for the case wherein neither a President elect nor a Vice President shall have qualified, declaring who shall then act as President, or the manner in which one who is to act shall be selected, and such person shall act accordingly until a President or Vice President shall have qualified. Section 4. The Congress may by law provide for the case of the death of any of the persons from whom the House of Representatives may choose a President whenever the right of choice shall have devolved upon them, and for the case of the death of any of the persons from whom the Senate may choose a Vice President whenever the right of choice shall have devolved upon them. Section 5. Sections 1 and 2 shall take effect on the 15th day of October following the ratification of this article. Section 6. This article shall be inoperative unless it shall have been ratified as an amendment to the Constitution by the legislatures of three-fourths of the several States within seven years from the date of its submission.*

= **Section 1** - "Lame Duck" amendment – changed date President takes office; **Section 2** – set timing of Congress' 1st meeting of the year…

21ˢᵗ Amendment (1933) *Section 1. The eighteenth article of amendment to the Constitution of the United States is hereby repealed.* **Section 2.** *The transportation or importation into any State, Territory, or Possession of the United States for delivery or use therein of intoxicating liquors, in violation of the laws thereof, is hereby prohibited.* **Section 3.** *This article shall be inoperative unless it shall have been ratified as an amendment to the Constitution by conventions in the several States, as provided in the Constitution, within seven years from the date of the submission hereof to the States by the Congress.*

= **Section 1** -- repealed 18ᵗʰ amendment; **Section 2** – gave states the power to legislate alcohol

22ⁿᵈ Amendment (1951) *Section 1. No person shall be elected to the office of the President more than twice, and no person who has held the office of President, or acted as President, for more than two years of a term to which some other person was elected President shall be elected to the office of President more than once. But this Article shall not apply to any person holding the office of President when this Article was proposed by Congress, and shall not prevent any person who may be holding the office of President, or acting as President, during the term within which this Article becomes operative from holding the office of President or acting as President during the remainder of such term.* **Section 2.** *This article shall be inoperative unless it shall have been ratified as an amendment to the Constitution by the legislatures of three-fourths of the several States within seven years from the date of its submission to the States by the Congress.*

= limited terms of president to 2 terms

23rd Amendment (1961) ***Section 1.*** *The District constituting the seat of Government of the United States shall appoint in such manner as Congress may direct: A number of electors of President and Vice President equal to the whole number of Senators and Representatives in Congress to which the District would be entitled if it were a State, but in no event more than the least populous State; they shall be in addition to those appointed by the States, but they shall be considered, for the purposes of the election of President and Vice President, to be electors appointed by a State; and they shall meet in the District and perform such duties as provided by the twelfth article of amendment.* ***Section 2.*** *The Congress shall have power to enforce this article by appropriate legislation.*

= D.C. citizens can now vote for president

24th Amendment (1964) ***Section 1.*** *The right of citizens of the United States to vote in any primary or other election for President or Vice President, for electors for President or Vice President, or for Senator or Representative in Congress, shall not be denied or abridged by the United States or any State by reason of failure to pay poll tax or other tax.* ***Section 2.*** *The Congress shall have power to enforce this article by appropriate legislation.*

= poll tax abolished

25th Amendment (1967) *Section 1. In case of the removal of the President from office or of his death or resignation, the Vice President shall become President.* **Section 2.** *Whenever there is a vacancy in the office of the Vice President, the President shall nominate a Vice President who shall take office upon confirmation by a majority vote of both Houses of Congress.* **Section 3.** *Whenever the President transmits to the President pro tempore of the Senate and the Speaker of the House of Representatives his written declaration that he is unable to discharge the powers and duties of his office, and until he transmits to them a written declaration to the contrary, such powers and duties shall be discharged by the Vice President as Acting President.* **Section 4.** *Whenever the Vice President and a majority of either the principal officers of the executive departments or of such other body as Congress may by law provide, transmit to the President pro tempore of the Senate and the Speaker of the House of Representatives their written declaration that the President is unable to discharge the powers and duties of his office, the Vice President shall immediately assume the powers and duties of the office as Acting President. Thereafter, when the President transmits to the President pro tempore of the Senate and the Speaker of the House of Representatives his written declaration that no inability exists, he shall resume the powers and duties of his office unless the Vice President and a majority of either the principal officers of the executive department or of such other body as Congress may by law provide, transmit within four days to the President pro tempore of the Senate and the Speaker of the House of Representatives their written declaration that the President is unable to discharge the powers and duties of his office. Thereupon Congress shall decide the issue, assembling within forty-eight hours for that purpose if not in session. If the Congress, within twenty-one days after receipt of the latter written declaration, or, if Congress is not in session, within twenty-one days after Congress is required to assemble, determines by two-thirds vote of both Houses that the President is unable to discharge the powers and duties of his office, the Vice President shall continue to discharge the same as Acting President; otherwise, the President shall resume the powers and duties of his office.*

= filling vacancy during term of president/vice-president

26th Amendment (1971) *Section 1. The right of citizens of the United States, who are eighteen years of age or older, to vote shall not be denied or abridged by the United States or by any State on account of age.* **Section 2.** *The Congress shall have power to enforce this article by appropriate legislation.*

=18 year olds can now vote

27th Amendment (1992) *No law, varying the compensation for the services of the Senators and Representatives, shall take effect, until an election of representatives shall have intervened.*

= can't change compensation during term of Congress (this amendment was 1st proposed in 1789)

Magna Carta, Excerpts from

(Originally signed in 1215)

(A translation of Magna Carta as confirmed by Edward I with his seal in 1297)

...Greeting. Know ye that we, unto the honour of Almighty God, and for the salvation of the souls of our progenitors and successors, Kings of England, to the advancement of holy Church, and amendment of our Realm, of our meer and free will, have given and granted to all Archbishops, Bishops, Abbots, Priors, Earls, Barons, and to all freemen of this our realm, these liberties following, to be kept in our kingdom of England for ever.

[1] First, We have granted to God, and by this our present Charter have confirmed, for us and our Heirs for ever, That the Church of England shall be free, and shall have her whole rights and liberties inviolable. We have granted also, and given to all the freemen of our realm, for us and our Heirs for ever, these liberties underwritten, to have and to hold to them and their Heirs, of us and our Heirs for ever...

...[8] We or our Bailiffs shall not seize any land or rent for any debt, as long as the present Goods and Chattels of the debtor do suffice to pay the debt, and the debtor himself be ready to satisfy therefore. Neither shall the pledges of the debtor be distrained, as long as the principal debtor is sufficient for the payment of the debt. And if the principal debtor fail in the payment of the debt, having nothing wherewith to pay, or will not pay where he is able, the pledges shall answer for the debt. And if they will, they shall have the lands and rents of the debtor, until they be satished of that which they before paid for him, except that the debtor can show himself to be acquitted against the said sureties...

…[13] Assises of Darrein Presentment shall be alway taken before our Justices of the Bench, and there shall be determined.

[14] A Freeman shall not be amerced for a small fault, but after the manner of the fault; and for a great fault after the greatness thereof, saving to him his contenement; and a Merchant likewise, saving to him his Merchandise; and any other's villain than ours shall be likewise amerced, saving his wainage, if he falls into our mercy. And none of the said amerciaments shall be assessed, but by the oath of honest and lawful men of the vicinage. Earls and Barons shall not be amerced but by their Peers, and after the manner of their offence. No man of the Church shall be amerced after the quantity of his spiritual Benefice, but after his Lay-tenement, and after the quantity of his offence…

…[20] No Constable shall distrain any Knight to give money for keeping of his Castle, if he himself will do it in his proper person, or cause it to be done by another sufficient man, if he may not do it himself for a reasonable cause. And if we lead or send him to an army, he shall be free from Castle-ward for the time that he shall be with us in fee in our host, for the which he hath done service in our wars.

[21] No Sheriff nor Bailiff of ours, or any other, shall take the Horses or Carts of any man to make carriage, except he pay the old price limited, that is to say, for carriage with two horse, x.d. a day; for three horse, xiv.d. a day. No demesne Cart of any Spiritual person or Knight, or any Lord, shall be taken by our Bailiffs; nor we, nor our Bailiffs, nor any other, shall take any man's wood for our Castles, or other our necessaries to be done, but by the licence of him whose wood it shall be…

…[28] No Bailiff from henceforth shall put any man to his open Law, nor to an Oath, upon his own bare saying, without faithful Witnesses brought in for the same.

[29] No Freeman shall be taken, or imprisoned, or be disseised of his Freehold, or Liberties, or free Customs, or be outlawed, or exiled, or any otherwise destroyed; nor will we pass upon him, nor condemn him, but by lawful Judgment of his Peers, or by the Law of the Land. We will sell to no man, we will not deny or defer to any man either Justice or Right…

The Mayflower Compact

(1620)

In the name of God, Amen. We, whose names are underwritten, the Loyal Subjects of our dread Sovereign Lord, King James, by the Grace of God, of England, France and Ireland, King, Defender of the Faith, e&.

Having undertaken for the Glory of God, and Advancement of the Christian Faith, and the Honour of our King and Country, a voyage to plant the first colony in the northern parts of Virginia; do by these presents, solemnly and mutually in the Presence of God and one of another, covenant and combine ourselves together into a civil Body Politick, for our better Ordering and Preservation, and Furtherance of the Ends aforesaid; And by Virtue hereof to enact, constitute, and frame, such just and equal Laws, Ordinances, Acts, Constitutions and Offices, from time to time, as shall be thought most meet and convenient for the General good of the Colony; unto which we promise all due submission and obedience.

In Witness whereof we have hereunto subscribed our names at Cape Cod the eleventh of November, in the Reign of our Sovereign Lord, King James of England, France and Ireland, the eighteenth, and of Scotland the fifty-fourth. Anno Domini, 1620.

Fundamental Orders of Connecticut,

Excerpts from (1639)

Forasmuch as it hath pleased the All-mighty God by the wise disposition of his divine providence so to Order and dispose of things that we the Inhabitants and Residents of Windsor, Hartford and Wethersfield are now cohabiting and dwelling in and upon the River of Connecticut and the Lands thereunto adjoining;

And well knowing where a people are gathered together the word of God requires that to maintain the peace and union of such a people there should be an orderly and decent Government established according to God, to order and dispose of the affairs of the people at all seasons as occasion shall require; do therefore associate and conjoin ourselves to be as one Public State or Commonwealth; and do, for ourselves and our Successors and such as shall be adjoined to us at any time hereafter, enter into Combination and Confederation together, to maintain and preserve the liberty and purity of the gospel of our Lord Jesus which we now profess, as also the discipline of the Churches, which according to the truth of the said gospel is now practiced amongst us;

As also in our Civil Affairs to be guided and governed according to such Laws, Rules, Orders and decrees as shall be made, ordered & decreed, as followeth:

1. It is Ordered...that there shall be yearly two general Assemblies or Courts, the one the second Thursday in April, the other the second Thursday in September, following; the first shall be called the Courte of Election, wherein shall be yearly chosen...so many Magistrates and other public Officers as shall be found requisite...

Massachusetts Body of Liberties, Excerpts from (1641)

The free fruition of such liberties, immunities, and privileges as humanity, civility, and Christianity call for as due to every man in his place and proportion without impeachment and infringement hath ever been and ever will be the tranquility and stability of churches and commonwealths. And the denial or deprival thereof, the disturbance if not the ruin of both.

We hold it, therefore, our duty and safety whilst we are about the further establishing of this government to collect and express all such freedoms as for present we foresee may concern us, and our posterity after us, and to ratify them with our solemn consent.

We do, therefore, this day religiously and unanimously decree and confirm these following rights, liberties, and privileges concerning our churches and civil state to be respectively, impartially, and inviolably enjoyed and observed throughout our jurisdiction forever.

1. No man's life shall be taken away, no man's honor or good name shall be stained, no man's person shall be arrested, restrained, banished, dismembered, nor any ways punished, no man shall be deprived of his wife or children, no man's goods or estate shall be taken away from him, nor any way damaged under color of law or countenance of authority, unless it be by virtue or equity of some express law of the country warranting the same, established by a general court and sufficiently published, or in case of the defect of a law in any particular case by the word of God…

2. Every person within this jurisdiction, whether inhabitant or foreigner, shall enjoy the same justice and law that is general for the plantation, which we constitute and execute one toward another without partiality or delay…

7. No man shall be compelled to go out of the limits of this plantation upon any offensive wars which this Commonwealth or any of our friends or confederates shall voluntarily undertake. But only upon such vindictive and defensive wars in our own behalf or the behalf of our friends and confederates as shall be enterprized by the counsel and consent of a court general, or by authority derived from the same.

8. No man's cattle or goods of what kind soever shall be pressed or taken for any public use or service, unless it be by warrant grounded upon some act of the General Court, nor without such reasonable prices and hire as the ordinary rates of the country do afford…

9. No monopolies shall be granted or allowed amongst us, but of such new inventions that are profitable to the country, and that for a short time…

17. Every man of, or within, this jurisdiction shall have free liberty, notwithstanding any civil power to remove both himself and his family at their pleasure out of the same, provided there be no legal impediment to the contrary.

RITES, RULES, AND LIBERTIES CONCERNING JUDICIAL PROCEEDINGS

18. No man's person shall be restrained or imprisoned by any authority whatsoever, before the law hath sentenced him thereto, if he can put in sufficient security, bail, or mainprise, for his appearance, and good behavior in the meantime, unless it be in crimes capital, and contempts in open court, and in such cases where some express act of court cloth allow it…

41. Every man that is to answer for any criminal cause, whether he be in prison or under bail, his cause shall be heard and determined at the next court that hath proper cognizance thereof and may be done without prejudice of justice.

42. No man shall be twice sentenced by civil justice for one and the same crime, offense, or trespass.

43. No man shall be beaten with above forty stripes, nor shall any true gentleman, nor any man equal to a gentleman be punished with whipping, unless his crime be very shameful, and his course of life vicious and profligate.

44. No man condemned to die shall be put to death within four days next after his condemnation, unless the court see special cause to the contrary…

45. No man shall be forced by torture to confess any crime against himself nor any other, unless it be in some capital case where he is first fully convicted by clear and sufficient evidence to be guilty, after which if the cause be of that nature, that it is very apparent there be other conspirators, or confederates with him, then he may be tortured, yet not with such tortures as be barbarous and inhumane.

46. For bodily punishments we allow amongst us none that are inhumane, barbarous, or cruel…

LIBERTIES MORE PECULIARLY CONCERNING THE FREEMEN…

LIBERTIES OF WOMEN…

LIBERTIES OF CHILDREN…

LIBERTIES OF SERVANTS…

LIBERTIES OF FOREIGNERS AND STRANGERS…

OF THE BRUTE CREATURE…

English Bill of Rights (1689)

An Act Declaring the Rights and Liberties of the Subject and Settling the Succession of the Crown

…Whereas the late King James the Second, by the assistance of divers evil counsellors, judges and ministers employed by him, did endeavour to subvert and extirpate the Protestant religion and the laws and liberties of this kingdom;

By assuming and exercising a power of dispensing with and suspending of laws and the execution of laws without consent of Parliament…

…By raising and keeping a standing army within this kingdom in time of peace without consent of Parliament, and quartering soldiers contrary to law…

…And whereas of late years partial corrupt and unqualified persons have been returned and served on juries in trials, and particularly divers jurors in trials for high treason which were not freeholders;

And excessive bail hath been required of persons committed in criminal cases to elude the benefit of the laws made for the liberty of the subjects;

And excessive fines have been imposed;

And illegal and cruel punishments inflicted…

…All which are utterly and directly contrary to the known laws and statutes and freedom of this realm…

...And thereupon the said Lords Spiritual and Temporal and Commons, pursuant to their respective letters and elections, being now assembled in a full and free representative of this nation, taking into their most serious consideration the best means for attaining the ends aforesaid, do in the first place (as their ancestors in like case have usually done) for the vindicating and asserting their ancient rights and liberties declare

That the pretended power of suspending the laws or the execution of laws by regal authority without consent of Parliament is illegal;

That the pretended power of dispensing with laws or the execution of laws by regal authority, as it hath been assumed and exercised of late, is illegal...

...That it is the right of the subjects to petition the king, and all commitments and prosecutions for such petitioning are illegal;

That the raising or keeping a standing army within the kingdom in time of peace, unless it be with consent of Parliament, is against law...

...That election of members of Parliament ought to be free;

That the freedom of speech and debates or proceedings in Parliament ought not to be impeached or questioned in any court or place out of Parliament;

That excessive bail ought not to be required, nor excessive fines imposed, nor cruel and unusual punishments inflicted;

That jurors ought to be duly impanelled and returned, and jurors which pass upon men in trials for high treason ought to be freeholders…

Resolutions of the Stamp Act
October 19, 1765

The members of this Congress, sincerely devoted, with the warmest sentiments of affection and duty to His Majesty's Person and Government, inviolably attached to the present happy establishment of the Protestant succession, and with minds deeply impressed by a sense of the present and impending misfortunes of the British colonies on this continent; having considered as maturely as time will permit the circumstances of the said colonies, esteem it our indispensable duty to make the following declarations of our humble opinion, respecting the most essential rights and liberties Of the colonists, and of the grievances under which they labour, by reason of several late Acts of Parliament.

I. That His Majesty's subjects in these colonies, owe the same allegiance to the Crown of Great-Britain, that is owing from his subjects born within the realm, and all due subordination to that august body the Parliament of Great Britain.

II. That His Majesty's liege subjects in these colonies, are entitled to all the inherent rights and liberties of his natural born subjects within the kingdom of Great-Britain.

III. That it is inseparably essential to the freedom of a people, and the undoubted right of Englishmen, that no taxes be imposed on them, but with their own consent, given personally, or by their representatives.

IV. That the people of these colonies are not, and from their local circumstances cannot be, represented in the House of Commons in Great-Britain.

V. That the only representatives of the people of these colonies, are persons chosen therein by themselves, and that no taxes ever have been, or can be constitutionally imposed on them, but by their respective legislatures.

VI. That all supplies to the Crown, being free gifts of the people, it is unreasonable and inconsistent with the principles and spirit of the British Constitution, for the people of Great-Britain to grant to His Majesty the property of the colonists.

VII. That trial by jury is the inherent and invaluable right of every British subject in these colonies.

VIII. That the late Act of Parliament, entitled, An Act for granting and applying certain Stamp Duties, and other Duties, in the British colonies and plantations in America, etc., by imposing taxes on the inhabitants of these colonies, and the said Act, and several other Acts, by extending the jurisdiction of the courts of Admiralty beyond its ancient limits, have a manifest tendency to subvert the rights and liberties of the colonists.

IX. That the duties imposed by several late Acts of Parliament, from the peculiar circumstances of these colonies, will be extremely burthensome and grievous; and from the scarcity of specie, the payment of them absolutely impracticable.

X. That as the profits of the trade of these colonies ultimately center in Great-Britain, to pay for the manufactures which they are obliged to take from thence, they eventually contribute very largely to all supplies granted there to the Crown.

XI. That the restrictions imposed by several late Acts of Parliament, on the trade of these colonies, will render them unable to purchase the manufactures of Great-Britain.

XII. That the increase, prosperity, and happiness of these colonies, depend on the full and free enjoyment of their rights and liberties, and an intercourse with Great-Britain mutually affectionate and advantageous.

XIII. That it is the right of the British subjects in these colonies, to petition the King, Or either House of Parliament.

Lastly, That it is the indispensable duty of these colonies, to the best of sovereigns, to the mother country, and to themselves, to endeavour by a loyal and dutiful address to his Majesty, and humble applications to both Houses of Parliament, to procure the repeal of the Act for granting and applying certain stamp duties, of all clauses of any other Acts of Parliament, whereby the jurisdiction of the Admiralty is extended as aforesaid, and of the other late Acts for the restriction of American commerce.

Fairfax County Resolves (July 18, 1774)

At a general Meeting of the Freeholders and Inhabitants of the County of Fairfax on Monday the 18th day of July 1774, at the Court House, George Washington Esquire Chairman, and Robert Harrison Gent. Clerk of the said Meeting--

1. Resolved that this Colony and Dominion of Virginia can not be considered as a conquered Country; and if it was, that the present Inhabitants are the Descendants not of the Conquered, but of the Conquerors.

That the same was not setled at the national Expence of England, but at the private Expence of the Adventurers, our Ancestors, by solemn Compact with, and under the Auspices and Protection of the British Crown; upon which we are in every Respect as dependant, as the People of Great Britain, and in the same Manner subject to all his Majesty's just, legal, and constitutional Prerogatives. That our Ancestors, when they left their native Land, and setled in America, brought with them (even if the same had not been confirmed by Charters) the Civil- Constitution and Form of Government of the Country they came from; and were by the Laws of Nature and Nations, entitled to all it's Privileges, Immunities and Advantages; which have descended to us their Posterity, and ought of Right to be as fully enjoyed, as if we had still continued within the Realm of England.

2. Resolved that the most important and valuable Part of the British Constitution, upon which it's very Existence depends, is the fundamental Principle of the People's being governed by no Laws, to which they have not given their Consent, by Representatives freely chosen by themselves; who are affected by the Laws they enact equally with their Constituents; to whom they are accountable, and whose Burthens they share; in which consists the Safety and Happiness of the Community: for if this Part of the Constitution was taken away, or materially altered, the Government must degenerate either into an absolute and despotic Monarchy, or a tyrannical Aristocracy, and the Freedom of the People be annihilated.

3. Resolved therefore, as the Inhabitants of the american Colonies are not, and from their situation can not be represented in the British Parliament, that the

legislative Power here can of Right be exercised only by {our} own Provincial Assemblys or Parliaments, subject to the Assent or Negative of the British Crown, to be declared within some proper limited Time.

But as it was thought just and reasonable that the People of Great Britain shou'd reap Advantages from these Colonies adequate to the Protection they afforded them, the British Parliament have claimed and exercised the Power of regulating our Trade and Commerce, so as to restrain our importing from foreign Countrys, such Articles as they cou'd furnish us with, of their own Growth or Manufacture, or exporting to foreign Countrys such Articles and Portions of our Produce, as Great Britain stood in Need of, for her won Consumption or Manufactures.

Such a Power directed with Wisdom and Moderation, seems necessary for the general Good of that great Body-politic of which we are a Part; altho' in some Degree repugnant to the Principles of the Constitution. Under this Idea our Ancestors submitted to it: the Experience of more than a Century, during the government of the reciprocal Benefits flowing from it produced mutual uninterrupted Harmony and Good- Will, between the Inhabitants of Great Britain and her Colonies; who during that long Period, always considered themselves as one and same People: and tho' such a Power is capable of Abuse, and in some Instances hath been stretched beyond the original Design and Institution.

Yet to avoid Strife and Contention with our fellow-Subjects, and strongly impressed with the Experience of mutual Benefits, we always Chearfully acquiesced in it, while the entire Regulation of our internal Policy, and giving and granting our own Money were preserved to our own provincial Legislatures.

4. Resolved that it is the Duty of these Colonies, on all Emergencies, to contribute, in Proportion to their Abilities, Situation and Circumstances, to the necessary Charge of supporting and defending the British Empire, of which they are Part; that while we are treated upon an equal Footing with our fellow Subjects, the Motives of Self-Interest and Preservation will be a sufficient Obligation; as was evident thro' the Course of the last War; and that no Argument can be fairly applyed to the British Parliament's taxing us, upon a

Presumption that we shou'd refuse a just and reasonable Contribution, but will equally operate in Justification of the Executive-Power taxing the People of England, upon a Supposition of their Representatives refusing to grant the necessary Supplies.

5. Resolved that the Claim lately assumed and exercised by the British Parliament, of making all such Laws as they think fit, to govern the People of these Colonies, and to extort from us our Money with out our Consent, is not only diametrically contrary to the first Principles of the Constitution, and the original Compacts by which we are dependant upon the British Crown and Government; but is totally incompatible with the Privileges of a free People, and the natural Rights of Mankind; will render our own Legislatures merely nominal and nugatory, and is calculated to reduce us from a State of Freedom and Happiness to Slavery and Misery.

6. Resolved that Taxation and Representation are in their Nature inseperable; that the Right of withholding, or of giving and granting their own Money is the only effectual Security to a free People, against the Incroachments of Despotism and Tyranny; and that whenever they yield the One, they must quickly fall a Prey to the other.

7. Resolved that the Powers over the People of America now claimed by the British House of Commons, in whose Election we have no Share, on whose Determinations we can have no Influence, whose Information mush be always defective and often false, who in many Instances may have a seperate, and in some an opposite Interest to ours, and who are removed from those Impressions of tenderness and compassion arising from personal intercourse and Connections, which soften the Rigours of the most despotic Governments, must if continued, establish the most grievous and intollerable Species of Tyranny and Oppression, that ever was inflicted upon Mankind.

8. Resolved that it is our greatest Wish and Inclination, as well as Interest, to continue our Connection with, and Dependance upon the British Government; but tho' we are it's Subjects, we will use every Means which Heaven hath given us to prevent our becoming it's Slaves.

9. Resolved that there is a premeditated Design and System, formed and pursued by the British Ministry, to introduce an arbitrary Government into his Majesty's American Diminions; to which End they are artfully prejudicing our Sovereign, and inflaming the Minds of our fellow-Subjects in Great Britain, by propagating the most malevolent Falsehoods; particularly that there is an Intention in the American Colonies to set up for independant States; endeavouring at the same Time, by various Acts of Violence and Oppression, by sudden and repeated Dissolutions of our Assemblies, whenever they presume to examine the Illegality of ministerial Mandates, or deliberate on the violated Rights of their Constituents, and by breaking in upon the American Charters, to reduce us to a State of Desperation, and dissolve the original Compacts by which our Ancestors bound themselves and their Posterity to remain dependant upon the British Crown: which Measures, unless effectually counteracted, will end in the Ruin both of Great Britain and her Colonies.

10. Resolved that the several Acts of Parliament for raising a Revenue upon the People of America without their Consent, the creating new and dangerous Jurisdictions here, the taking away our Trials by Jurys, the ordering Persons upon Criminal Accusations, to be tried in another Country than that in which the Fact is charged to have been committed, the Act inflicting ministerial Vengeance upon the Town of Boston, and the two Bills lately brought into Parliament for abrogating the Charter of the Province of Massachusetts Bay, and for the Protection and Encouragement of Murderers in the said Province, are Part of the above mentioned iniquitous System.

That the Inhabitants of the Town of Boston are now suffering in the common Cause of all British America, and are justly entitled to it's Support and Assistance; and therefore that a Subscription ought imediatly to be opened, and proper Persons appointed, in every County of this Colony to purchase Provisions, and consign them to some Gentleman of Character in Boston, to be distributed among the poorer Sort of People there.

11. Resolved that we will cordially join with our Friends and Brethren of this and the other Colonies, in such Measures as shall be judged most effectual for procuring Redress of our Grievances, and that upon obtaining such Redress if the Destruction of the Tea at Boston be regarded as an Invasion of private

Property, we shall be willing to contribute towards paying the East India Company the Value: but as we consider the said Company as the Tools and Instrument of Oppression in the Hands of Government and the Cause of our present Distress, it is the Opinion of this Meeting that the People of these Colonies shou'd forbear all further Dealings with them, by refusing to purchase their Merchandize, until that Peace Safety and Good- order, which they have disturbed, be perfectly restored.

And that all Tea now in this Colony, or which shall be imported into it shiped before the first Day of September next, shou'd be deposited in some Storehouse to be appointed by the respective Committees of each County, until a sufficient Sum of Money be raised by Subscription to reimburse the Owners the Value, and then to be publickly burn'd and destroyed; and if the same is not paid for and destroyed as aforesaid, that it remain in the Custody of the said Committees, at the Risque of the Owners, until the Act of Parliament imposing a Duty upon Tea for raising a Revenue in America be repealed; and imediatly afterwards be delivered unto the several Proprietors thereof, their Agents or Attorneys.

12. Resolved that Nothing will so much contribute to defeat the pernicious Designs of the common Enemies of Great Britain and her Colonies as a firm Union of the latter; who ought to regard every Act of Violence or Oppression inflicted upon any one of them, as aimed at all; and to effect this desireable Purpose, that a Congress shou'd be appointed, to consist of Deputies from all the Colonies, to concert a general and uniform Plan for the Defence and Preservation of our common Rights, and continueing the Connection and Dependance of the said Colonies upon Great Britain under a just, lenient, permanent, and constitutional Form of Government.

13. Resolved that our most sincere and cordial Thanks be given to the Patrons and Friends of Liberty in Great Britain, for their spirited and patriotick Conduct in Support of our constitutional Rights and Privileges, and their generous Efforts to prevent the present Distress and Calamity of America.

14. Resolved that every little jarring Interest and Dispute, which has ever happened between these Colonies, shou'd be buried in eternal Oblivion; that all Manner of Luxury and Extravagance ought imediatly to be laid aside, as totally

inconsistent with the threatening and gloomy Prospect before us; that it is the indispensable Duty of all the Gentlemen and Men of Fortune to set Examples of Temperance, Fortitude, Frugality and Industry; and give every Encouragement in their Power, particularly by Subscriptions and Premiums, to the Improvement of Arts and Manufactures in America; that great Care and Attention shou'd be had to the Cultivation of Flax, Cotton, and other Materials for Manufactures; and we recommend it to such of the Inhabitants who have large Stocks of Sheep, to sell to their Neighbors at a moderate Price, as the most certain Means of speedily increasing our Breed of Sheep, and Quantity of Wool.

15. Resolved that until American Grievances be redressed, by Restoration of our just Rights and Privileges, no Goods or Merchandize whatsoever ought to be imported into this Colony, which shall be shiped from Great Britain or Ireland after the first Day of September next, except Linnens not exceeding fifteen Pence {per} yard, coarse woolen Cloth, not exceeding two Shillings sterling {per} Yard, Nails Wire, and Wire-Cards, Needles & Pins, Paper, Salt Petre, and Medecines; which may {which three Articles only may} be imported until the first Day of September, one thousand seven hundred and seventy six; and if any Goods or Merchandize, othe[r] than those hereby excepted, shou'd be ship'd from Great Britain, {or Ireland} after the time aforesaid, to this Colony, that the same, immediately upon their Arrival, shou'd either be sent back again, by the Owners their Agents or Attorn[ey]s, or stored and deposited in some Ware- house, to be appointed by the Committee for each respective County, and there kept, at the Risque and Charge of the Owners, to be delivered to them, when a free Importation of Goods hither shall again take Place.

And that the Merchants and Venders of Goods and Merchandize within this Colony ought not to take Advantage of our present Distress b[u]t continue to sell the Goods and Merchandize which they now have, or which may be shiped to them before the first Day of September next, at the same Rates and Prices they have been accustomed to do, within one Year last past; and if any Person shall sell such Goods on any other Terms than above expressed, that no Inhabitant of this Colony shou'd at any time, for ever thereafter, deal with him, his Agent, Factor, or Store keepers for any Commodity whatsoever.

16. Resolved that it is the Opinion of this Meeting, that the Merchants and Venders of Goods and Merchandize within this Colony shou'd take an Oath, not to sell or dispose of any Goods or Merchandize whatsoever, which may be shiped from Great Britain {or Ireland} after the first Day of September next as aforesaid, except the {three} Articles before excepted, and that they will, upon Receipt of such prohibited Goods, either send the same back again by the first Opportunity, or deliver them to the Committees in the respective Countys, to be deposited in some Warehouse, at the Risque and Charge of the Owners, until they, their Agents or Factors be permitted to take them away by the said Committees: the Names of those who refuse to take such Oath to be advertized by the respective Committees in the Countys wherein they reside., And to the End that the Inhabitants of this Colony may know what Merchants, and Venders of Goods and Merchandize have taken such Oath, that the respective Committees shou'd grant a Certificate thereof to every such Person who shall take the same.

17. Resolved that it is the Opinion of this Meeting, that during our present Difficulties and Distress, no Slaves ought to be imported into any of the British Colonies on this Continent; and we take this Opportunity of declaring our most earnest Wishes to see an entire Stop for ever put to such a wicked cruel and unnatural Trade.

18. Resolved that no kind of Lumber shou'd be exported from this Colony to the West Indies, until America be restored to her constitutional Rights and Liberties if the other Colonies will accede to a like Resolution; and that it be recommended to the general Congress to appoint as early a Day as possible for stopping such Export.

19. Resolved that it is the Opinion of this Meeting, if American Grievances be not redressed before the first Day of November one thousand seven hundred and seventy five, that all Exports of Produce from the several Colonies to Great Britain {or Ireland} shou'd cease; and to carry the said Resolution more effectually into Execution, that we will not plant or cultivate any Tobacco, after the Crop now growing; provided the same Measure shall be adopted by the other Colonies on this Continent, as well those who have heretofore made Tobacco, as those who have not.

And it is our Opinion also, if the Congress of Deputies from the several Colonies shall adopt the Measure of Non- exportation to Great Britain, as the People will be thereby disabled from paying their Debts, that no Judgements shou'd be rendered by the Courts in the said Colonies for any Debt, after Information of the said Measure's being determined upon.

20. Resolved that it is the Opinion of this Meeting that a solemn Covenant and Association shou'd be entered into by the Inhabitants of all the Colonies upon Oath, that they will not, after the Times which shall be respectively agreed on at the general Congress, export any Manner of Lumber to the West Indies, nor any of their Produce to Great Britain {or Ireland}, or sell or dispose of the same to any Person who shall not have entered into the said Covenant and Association; and also that they will no import or receive any Goods or Merchandize which shall be ship'd from Great Britain {or Ireland} after the first Day of September next, other than the before enumerated Articles, nor buy or purchase any Goods, except as before excepted, of any Person whatsoever, who shall not have taken the Oath herein before recommended to be taken by the Merchants and Venders of Goods nor buy or purchase any Slaves hereafter imported into any Part of this Continent until a free Exportation and Importation be again resolved on by a Majority of the Representatives or Deputies of the Colonies.

And that the respective Committees of the Countys, in each Colony so soon as the Covenant and Association becomes general, publich by Advertisements in their several Counties {and Gazettes of their Colonies}, a List of the Names of those (if any such there be) who will not accede thereto; that such Traitors to their Country may be publickly known and detested.

21. Resolved that it is the Opinion of this Meeting, that this and the other associating Colonies shou'd break off all Trade, Intercourse, and Dealings, with that Colony Province or Town which shall decline or refuse to agree to the Plan which shall be adopted by the general Congress.

22. Resolved that shou'd the Town of Boston be forced to submit to the late cruel and oppressive Measures of Government, that we shall not hold the same to be binding upon us, but will, notwithstanding , religiously maintain, and

inviolably adhere to such Measures as shall be concerted by the general Congress, for the preservation of our Lives Liberties and Fortunes.

23. Resolved that it be recommended to the Deputies of the general Congress to draw up and transmit an humble and dutiful Petition and Remonstrance to his Majesty, asserting with decent Firmness our just and constitutional Rights and Privileg[es,] lamenting the fatal Necessity of being compelled to enter into Measur[es] disgusting to his Majesty and his Parliament, or injurious to our fellow Subjects in Great Britain; declaring, in the strongest Terms, ou[r] Duty and Affection to his Majesty's Person, Family [an]d Government, and our Desire to continue our Dependance upon Great Bri[tai]n; and most humbly conjuring and beseeching his Majesty, not to reduce his faithful Subjects of America to a State of desperation, and to reflect, that from our Sovereign there can be but one Appeal. And it is the Opinion of this Meeting, that after such Petition and Remonstrance shall have been presented to his Majesty, the same shou'd be printed in the public Papers, in all the principal Towns in Great Britain.

24. Resolved that George Washington Esquire, and George Broadwater Gent. lately elected our Representatives to serve in the general Assembly, be appointed to attend the Convention at Williamsburg on the first Day of August next, and present these Resolves, as the Sense of the People of this County, upon the Measures proper to be taken in the present alarming and dangerous Situation of America.

Give Me Liberty or Give Me Death (1775)
by Patrick Henry

No man thinks more highly than I do of the patriotism, as well as abilities, of the very worthy gentlemen who have just addressed the house. But different men often see the same subject in different lights; and, therefore, I hope it will not be thought disrespectful to those gentlemen if, entertaining as I do opinions of a character very opposite to theirs, I shall speak forth my sentiments freely and without reserve. This is no time for ceremony. The question before the house is one of awful moment to this country.

For my own part, I consider it as nothing less than a question of freedom or slavery; and in proportion to the magnitude of the subject ought to be the freedom of the debate. It is only in this way that we can hope to arrive at the truth, and fulfill the great responsibility which we hold to God and our country. Should I keep back my opinions at such a time, through fear of giving offense, I should consider myself as guilty of treason towards my country, and of an act of disloyalty toward the Majesty of Heaven, which I revere above all earthly kings.

Mr. President, it is natural to man to indulge in the illusions of hope. We are apt to shut our eyes against a painful truth, and listen to the song of that siren till she transforms us into beasts. Is this the part of wise men, engaged in a great and arduous struggle for liberty? Are we disposed to be of the numbers of those who, having eyes, see not, and, having ears, hear not, the things which so nearly concern their temporal salvation? For my part, whatever anguish of spirit it may cost, I am willing to know the whole truth, to know the worst, and to provide for it.

I have but one lamp by which my feet are guided, and that is the lamp of experience. I know of no way of judging of the future but by the past. And judging by the past, I wish to know what there has been in the conduct of the British ministry for the last ten years to justify those hopes with which gentlemen have been pleased to solace themselves and the House. Is it that insidious smile with which our petition has been lately received?

Trust it not, sir; it will prove a snare to your feet. Suffer not yourselves to be betrayed with a kiss. Ask yourselves how this gracious reception of our petition comports with those warlike preparations which cover our waters and darken our land. Are fleets and armies necessary to a work of love and reconciliation? Have we shown ourselves so unwilling to be reconciled that force must be called in to win back our love?

Let us not deceive ourselves, sir. These are the implements of war and subjugation; the last arguments to which kings resort. I ask gentlemen, sir, what means this martial array, if its purpose be not to force us to submission? Can gentlement assign any other possible motive for it?

Has Great Britain any enemy, in this quarter of the world, to call for all this accumulation of navies and armies? No, sir, she has none. They are meant for us: they can be meant for no other. They are sent over to bind and rivet upon us those chains which the British ministry have been so long forging. And what have we to oppose to them? Shall we try argument? Sir, we have been trying that for the last ten years.

Have we anything new to offer upon the subject? Nothing. We have held the subject up in every light of which it is capable; but it has been all in vain. Shall we resort to entreaty and humble supplication? What terms shall we find which have not been already exhausted? Let us not, I beseech you, sir, deceive ourselves. Sir, we have done everything that could be done to avert the storm which is now coming on.

We have petitioned; we have remonstrated; we have supplicated; we have prostrated ourselves before the throne, and have implored its interposition to arrest the tyrannical hands of the ministry and Parliament. Our petitions have been slighted; our remonstrances have produced additional violence and insult; our supplications have been disregarded; and we have been spurned, with contempt, from the foot of the throne! In vain, after these things, may we indulge the fond hope of peace and reconciliation.

There is no longer any room for hope. If we wish to be free--if we mean to preserve inviolate those inestimable privileges for which we have been so long contending--if we mean not basely to abandon the noble struggle in which we have been so long engaged, and which we have pledged ourselves never to abandon until the glorious object of our contest shall be obtained--we must fight! I repeat it, sir, we must fight!

An appeal to arms and to the God of hosts is all that is left us! They tell us, sir, that we are weak; unable to cope with so formidable an adversary. But when shall we be stronger? Will it be the next week, or the next year? Will it be when we are totally disarmed, and when a British guard shall be stationed in every house? Shall we gather strength but irresolution and inaction? Shall we acquire the means of effectual resistance by lying supinely on our backs and hugging the delusive phantom of hope, until our enemies shall have bound us hand and foot?

Sir, we are not weak if we make a proper use of those means which the God of nature hath placed in our power. The millions of people, armed in the holy cause of liberty, and in such a country as that which we possess, are invincible by any force which our enemy can send against us. Besides, sir, we shall not fight our battles alone. There is a just God who presides over the destinies of nations, and who will raise up friends to fight our battles for us. The battle, sir, is not to the strong alone; it is to the vigilant, the active, the brave.

Besides, sir, we have no election. If we were base enough to desire it, it is now too late to retire from the contest. There is no retreat but in submission and slavery! Our chains are forged! Their clanking may be heard on the plains of Boston! The war is inevitable--and let it come! I repeat it, sir, let it come.

It is in vain, sir, to extentuate the matter. Gentlemen may cry, Peace, Peace--but there is no peace. The war is actually begun! The next gale that sweeps from the north will bring to our ears the clash of resounding arms! Our brethren are already in the field! Why stand we here idle? What is it that gentlemen wish? What would they have? Is life so dear, or peace so sweet, as to be purchased at the price of chains and slavery? Forbid it, Almighty God! I know not what course others may take; but as for me, give me liberty or give me death!

Declaration of the Causes and Necessity of Taking Up Arms (July 6, 1775)

A declaration by the representatives of the united colonies of North America, now met in Congress at Philadelphia, setting forth the causes and necessity of their taking up arms.

If it was possible for men, who exercise their reason to believe, that the divine Author of our existence intended a part of the human race to hold an absolute property in, and an unbounded power over others, marked out by his infinite goodness and wisdom, as the objects of a legal domination never rightfully resistible, however severe and oppressive, the inhabitants of these colonies might at least require from the parliament of Great-Britain some evidence, that this dreadful authority over them, has been granted to that body.

But a reverance for our Creator, principles of humanity, and the dictates of common sense, must convince all those who reflect upon the subject, that government was instituted to promote the welfare of mankind, and ought to be administered for the attainment of that end. The legislature of Great-Britain, however, stimulated by an inordinate passion for a power not only unjustifiable, but which they know to be peculiarly reprobated by the very constitution of that kingdom, and desparate of success in any mode of contest, where regard should be had to truth, law, or right, have at length, deserting those, attempted to effect their cruel and impolitic purpose of enslaving these colonies by violence, and have thereby rendered it necessary for us to close with their last appeal from reason to arms.

Yet, however blinded that assembly may be, by their intemperate rage for unlimited domination, so to sight justice and the opinion of mankind, we esteem ourselves bound by obligations of respect to the rest of the world, to make known the justice of our cause. Our forefathers, inhabitants of the island of Great-Britain, left their native land, to seek on these shores a residence for civil and religious freedom.

At the expense of their blood, at the hazard of their fortunes, without the least charge to the country from which they removed, by unceasing labour, and an unconquerable spirit, they effected settlements in the distant and unhospitable wilds of America, then filled with numerous and warlike barbarians. -- Societies or governments, vested with perfect legislatures, were formed under charters from the crown, and an harmonious intercourse was established between the colonies and the kingdom from which they derived their origin.

The mutual benefits of this union became in a short time so extraordinary, as to excite astonishment. It is universally confessed, that the amazing increase of the wealth, strength, and navigation of the realm, arose from this source; and the minister, who so wisely and successfully directed the measures of Great-Britain in the late war, publicly declared, that these colonies enabled her to triumph over her enemies. --Towards the conclusion of that war, it pleased our sovereign to make a change in his counsels. -- From that fatal movement, the affairs of the British empire began to fall into confusion, and gradually sliding from the summit of glorious prosperity, to which they had been advanced by the virtues and abilities of one man, are at length distracted by the convulsions, that now shake it to its deepest foundations. -- The new ministry finding the brave foes of Britain, though frequently defeated, yet still contending, took up the unfortunate idea of granting them a hasty peace, and then subduing her faithful friends.

These colonies were judged to be in such a state, as to present victories without bloodshed, and all the easy emoluments of statuteable plunder. -- The uninterrupted tenor of their peaceable and respectful behaviour from the beginning of colonization, their dutiful, zealous, and useful services during the war, though so recently and amply acknowledged in the most honourable manner by his majesty, by the late king, and by parliament, could not save them from the meditated innovations. -- Parliament was influenced to adopt the pernicious project, and assuming a new power over them, have in the course of eleven years, given such decisive specimens of the spirit and consequences attending this power, as to leave no doubt concerning the effects of acquiescence under it.

They have undertaken to give and grant our money without our consent, though we have ever exercised an exclusive right to dispose of our own property; statutes have been passed for extending the jurisdiction of courts of admiralty and vice-admiralty beyond their ancient limits; for depriving us of the accustomed and inestimable privilege of trial by jury, in cases affecting both life and property; for suspending the legislature of one of the colonies; for interdicting all commerce to the capital of another; and for altering fundamentally the form of government established by charter, and secured by acts of its own legislature solemnly confirmed by the crown; for exempting the "murderers" of colonists from legal trial, and in effect, from punishment; for erecting in a neighbouring province, acquired by the joint arms of Great-Britain and America, a despotism dangerous to our very existence; and for quartering soldiers upon the colonists in time of profound peace.

It has also been resolved in parliament, that colonists charged with committing certain offences, shall be transported to England to be tried. But why should we enumerate our injuries in detail? By one statute it is declared, that parliament can "of right make laws to bind us in all cases whatsoever." What is to defend us against so enormous, so unlimited a power? Not a single man of those who assume it, is chosen by us; or is subject to our control or influence; but, on the contrary, they are all of them exempt from the operation of such laws, and an American revenue, if not diverted from the ostensible purposes for which it is raised, would actually lighten their own burdens in proportion, as they increase ours.

We saw the misery to which such despotism would reduce us. We for ten years incessantly and ineffectually besieged the throne as supplicants; we reasoned, we remonstrated with parliament, in the most mild and decent language.

Administration sensible that we should regard these oppressive measures as freemen ought to do, sent over fleets and armies to enforce them. The indignation of the Americans was roused, it is true; but it was the indignation of a virtuous, loyal, and affectionate people. A Congress of delegates from the United Colonies was assembled at Philadelphia, on the fifth day of last September. We resolved again to offer an humble and dutiful petition to the King, and also addressed our fellow-subjects of Great-Britain.

We have pursued every temperate, every respectful measure; we have even proceeded to break off our commercial intercourse with our fellow-subjects, as the last peaceable admonition, that our attachment to no nation upon earth should supplant our attachment to liberty. -- This, we flattered ourselves, was the ultimate step of the controversy: but subsequent events have shewn, how vain was this hope of finding moderation in our enemies.

Several threatening expressions against the colonies were inserted in his majesty's speech; our petition, tho' we were told it was a decent one, and that his majesty had been pleased to receive it graciously, and to promise laying it before his parliament, was huddled into both houses among a bundle of American papers, and there neglected. The lords and commons in their address, in the month of February, said, that "a rebellion at that time actually existed within the province of Massachusetts- Bay; and that those concerned with it, had been countenanced and encouraged by unlawful combinations and engagements, entered into by his majesty's subjects in several of the other colonies; and therefore they besought his majesty, that he would take the most effectual measures to inforce due obediance to the laws and authority of the supreme legislature." -- Soon after, the commercial intercourse of whole colonies, with foreign countries, and with each other, was cut off by an act of parliament; by another several of them were intirely prohibited from the fisheries in the seas near their coasts, on which they always depended for their sustenance; and large reinforcements of ships and troops were immediately sent over to general Gage.

Fruitless were all the entreaties, arguments, and eloquence of an illustrious band of the most distinguished peers, and commoners, who nobly and strenuously asserted the justice of our cause, to stay, or even to mitigate the heedless fury with which these accumulated and unexampled outrages were hurried on. -- equally fruitless was the interference of the city of London, of Bristol, and many other respectable towns in our favor.

Parliament adopted an insidious manoeuvre calculated to divide us, to establish a perpetual auction of taxations where colony should bid against colony, all of them uninformed what ransom would redeem their lives; and thus to extort from us, at the point of the bayonet, the unknown sums that should be sufficient to gratify, if possible to gratify, ministerial rapacity, with the miserable indulgence left to us of raising, in our own mode, the prescribed tribute. What terms more rigid and humiliating could have been dictated by remorseless victors to conquered enemies? in our circumstances to accept them, would be to deserve them.

Soon after the intelligence of these proceedings arrived on this continent, general Gage, who in the course of the last year had taken possession of the town of Boston, in the province of Massachusetts-Bay, and still occupied it a garrison, on the 19th day of April, sent out from that place a large detachment of his army, who made an unprovoked assault on the inhabitants of the said province, at the town of Lexington, as appears by the affidavits of a great number of persons, some of whom were officers and soldiers of that detachment, murdered eight of the inhabitants, and wounded many others.

From thence the troops proceeded in warlike array to the town of Concord, where they set upon another party of the inhabitants of the same province, killing several and wounding more, until compelled to retreat by the country people suddenly assembled to repel this cruel aggression. Hostilities, thus commenced by the British troops, have been since prosecuted by them without regard to faith or reputation. -- The inhabitants of Boston being confined within that town by the general their governor, and having, in order to procure their dismission, entered into a treaty with him, it was stipulated that the said inhabitants having deposited their arms with their own magistrate, should have liberty to depart, taking with them their other effects.

They accordingly delivered up their arms, but in open violation of honour, in defiance of the obligation of treaties, which even savage nations esteemed sacred, the governor ordered the arms deposited as aforesaid, that they might be preserved for their owners, to be seized by a body of soldiers; detained the greatest part of the inhabitants in the town, and compelled the few who were permitted to retire, to leave their most valuable effects behind.

By this perfidy wives are separated from their husbands, children from their parents, the aged and the sick from their relations and friends, who wish to attend and comfort them; and those who have been used to live in plenty and even elegance, are reduced to deplorable distress.

The general, further emulating his ministerial masters, by a proclamation bearing date on the 12th day of June, after venting the grossest falsehoods and calumnies against the good people of these colonies, proceeds to "declare them all, either by name or description, to be rebels and traitors, to supercede the course of the common law, and instead thereof to publish and order the use and exercise of the law martial." -- His troops have butchered our countrymen, have wantonly burnt Charlestown, besides a considerable number of houses in other places; our ships and vessels are seized; the necessary supplies of provisions are intercepted, and he is exerting his utmost power to spread destruction and devastation around him.

We have rceived certain intelligence, that general Carleton, the governor of Canada, is instigating the people of that province and the Indians to fall upon us; and we have but too much reason to apprehend, that schemes have been formed to excite domestic enemies against us. In brief, a part of these colonies now feel, and all of them are sure of feeling, as far as the vengeance of administration can inflict them, the complicated calamities of fire, sword and famine. [1] We are reduced to the alternative of chusing an unconditional submission to the tyranny of irritated ministers, or resistance by force. -- The latter is our choice. –

We have counted the cost of this contest, and find nothing so dreadful as voluntary slavery. -- Honour, justice, and humanity, forbid us tamely to surrender that freedom which we received from our gallant ancestors, and which our innocent posterity have a right to receive from us. We cannot endure the infamy and guilt of resigning succeeding generations to that wretchedness which inevitably awaits them, if we basely entail hereditary bondage upon them.

Our cause is just. Our union is perfect. Our internal resources are great, and, if necessary, foreign assistance is undoubtedly attainable. -- We gratefully acknowledge, as signal instances of the Divine favour towards us, that his Providence would not permit us to be called into this severe controversy, until we were grown up to our present strength, had been previously exercised in warlike operation, and possessed of the means of defending ourselves.

With hearts fortified with these animating reflections, we most solemnly, before God and the world, declare, that, exerting the utmost energy of those powers, which our beneficent Creator hath graciously bestowed upon us, the arms we have been compelled by our enemies to assume, we will, in defiance of every hazard, with unabating firmness and perseverence, employ for the preservation of our liberties; being with one mind resolved to die freemen rather than to live slaves.

Lest this declaration should disquiet the minds of our friends and fellow-subjects in any part of the empire, we assure them that we mean not to dissolve that union which has so long and so happily subsisted between us, and which we sincerely wish to see restored. -- Necessity has not yet driven us into that desperate measure, or induced us to excite any other nation to war against them. -- We have not raised armies with ambitious designs of separating from Great-Britain, and establishing independent states.

We fight not for glory or for conquest. We exhibit to mankind the remarkable spectacle of a people attacked by unprovoked enemies, without any imputation or even suspicion of offence. They boast of their privileges and civilization, and yet proffer no milder conditions than servitude or death.

In our own native land, in defence of the freedom that is our birthright, and which we ever enjoyed till the late violation of it -- for the protection of our property, acquired solely by the honest industry of our fore-fathers and ourselves, against violence actually offered, we have taken up arms. We shall lay them down when hostilities shall cease on the part of the aggressors, and all danger of their being renewed shall be removed, and not before.

With an humble confidence in the mercies of the supreme and impartial Judge and Ruler of the Universe, we most devoutly implore his divine goodness to protect us happily through this great conflict, to dispose our adversaries to reconciliation on reasonable terms, and thereby to relieve the empire from the calamities of civil war.

Common Sense, Excerpts from
by Thomas Paine (January/February 1776)

Of the Origin and Design of Government in General, with Concise Remarks on the English Constitution

SOME writers have so confounded society with government, as to leave little or no distinction between them; whereas they are not only different, but have different origins. Society is produced by our wants, and government by our wickedness; the former promotes our happiness POSITIVELY by uniting our affections, the latter NEGATIVELY by restraining our vices. The one encourages intercourse, the other creates distinctions. The first is a patron, the last a punisher.

Society in every state is a blessing, but Government, even in its best state, is but a necessary evil; in its worst state an intolerable one: for when we suffer, or are exposed to the same miseries BY A GOVERNMENT, which we might expect in a country WITHOUT GOVERNMENT, our calamity is heightened by reflecting that we furnish the means by which we suffer.

Government, like dress, is the badge of lost innocence; the palaces of kings are built upon the ruins of the bowers of paradise. For were the impulses of conscience clear, uniform and irresistibly obeyed, man would need no other lawgiver; but that not being the case, he finds it necessary to surrender up a part of his property to furnish means for the protection of the rest; and this he is induced to do by the same prudence which in every other case advises him, out of two evils to choose the least. Wherefore, security being the true design and end of government, it unanswerably follows that whatever form thereof appears most likely to ensure it to us, with the least expense and greatest benefit, is preferable to all others…

…Here then is the origin and rise of government; namely, a mode rendered necessary by the inability of moral virtue to govern the world; here too is the design and end of government, viz. Freedom and security. And however our eyes may be dazzled with show, or our ears deceived by sound; however prejudice may warp our wills, or interest darken our understanding, the simple voice of nature and reason will say, 'tis right.

I draw my idea of the form of government from a principle in nature which no art can overturn, viz. that the more simple any thing is, the less liable it is to be disordered, and the easier repaired when disordered; and with this maxim in view I offer a few remarks on the so much boasted constitution of England. That it was noble for the dark and slavish times in which it was erected, is granted. When the world was overrun with tyranny the least remove there from was a glorious rescue. But that it is imperfect, subject to convulsions, and incapable of producing what it seems to promise is easily demonstrated.

Absolute governments, (tho' the disgrace of human nature) have this advantage with them, they are simple; if the people suffer, they know the head from which their suffering springs; know likewise the remedy; and are not bewildered by a variety of causes and cures. But the constitution of England is so exceedingly complex, that the nation may suffer for years together without being able to discover in which part the fault lies; some will say in one and some in another, and every political physician will advise a different medicine.

I know it is difficult to get over local or long standing prejudices, yet if we will suffer ourselves to examine the component parts of the English Constitution, we shall find them to be the base remains of two ancient tyrannies, compounded with some new Republican materials.

First. — The remains of Monarchical tyranny in the person of the King.

Secondly. — The remains of Aristocratical tyranny in the persons of the Peers.

Thirdly. — The new Republican materials, in the persons of the Commons, on whose virtue depends the freedom of England.

The two first, by being hereditary, are independent of the People; wherefore in a CONSTITUTIONAL SENSE they contribute nothing towards the freedom of the State.

To say that the constitution of England is an UNION of three powers, reciprocally CHECKING each other, is farcical; either the words have no meaning, or they are flat contradictions.

First. — That the King it not to be trusted without being looked after; or in other words, that a thirst for absolute power is the natural disease of monarchy.

Secondly. — That the Commons, by being appointed for that purpose, are either wiser or more worthy of confidence than the Crown.

But as the same constitution which gives the Commons a power to check the King by withholding the supplies, gives afterwards the King a power to check the Commons, by empowering him to reject their other bills; it again supposes that the King is wiser than those whom it has already supposed to be wiser than him. A mere absurdity!

There is something exceedingly ridiculous in the composition of Monarchy; it first excludes a man from the means of information, yet empowers him to act in cases where the highest judgment is required. The state of a king shuts him from the World, yet the business of a king requires him to know it thoroughly; wherefore the different parts, by unnaturally opposing and destroying each other, prove the whole character to be absurd and useless…

…Wherefore, laying aside all national pride and prejudice in favour of modes and forms, the plain truth is that IT IS WHOLLY OWING TO THE CONSTITUTION OF THE PEOPLE, AND NOT TO THE CONSTITUTION OF THE GOVERNMENT that the crown is not as oppressive in England as in Turkey.

…Thoughts on the Present State of American Affairs

…Volumes have been written on the subject of the struggle between England and America. Men of all ranks have embarked in the controversy, from different motives, and with various designs; but all have been ineffectual, and the period of debate is closed. Arms as the last resource decide the contest; the appeal was the choice of the King, and the Continent has accepted the challenge…

…The Sun never shined on a cause of greater worth. 'Tis not the affair of a City, a County, a Province, or a Kingdom; but of a Continent — of at least one-eighth part of the habitable Globe. 'Tis not the concern of a day, a year, or an age; posterity are virtually involved in the contest, and will be more or less affected even to the end of time, by the proceedings now. Now is the seed-time of Continental union, faith and honour. The least fracture now will be like a name engraved with the point of a pin on the tender rind of a young oak; the wound would enlarge with the tree, and posterity read in it full grown characters…

..I have heard it asserted by some, that as America has flourished under her former connection with Great Britain, the same connection is necessary towards her future happiness, and will always have the same effect. Nothing can be more fallacious than this kind of argument. We may as well assert that because a child has thrived upon milk, that it is never to have meat, or that the first twenty years of our lives is to become a precedent for the next twenty. But even this is admitting more than is true; for I answer roundly that America would have flourished as much, and probably much more, had no European power taken any notice of her. The commerce by which she hath enriched herself are the necessaries of life, and will always have a market while eating is the custom of Europe.

But she has protected us, say some. That she hath engrossed us is true, and defended the Continent at our expense as well as her own, is admitted; and she would have defended Turkey from the same motive, viz. — for the sake of trade and dominion…

…It hath lately been asserted in parliament, that the Colonies have no relation to each other but through the Parent Country, i.e. that Pennsylvania and the Jerseys and so on for the rest, are sister Colonies by the way of England; this is certainly a very roundabout way of proving relationship, but it is the nearest and only true way of proving enmity (or enemyship, if I may so call it.) France and Spain never were, nor perhaps ever will be, our enemies as AMERICANS, but as our being the SUBJECTS OF GREAT BRITAIN…

…But, admitting that we were all of English descent, what does it amount to? Nothing. Britain, being now an open enemy, extinguishes every other name and title: and to say that reconciliation is our duty, is truly farcical. The first king of England, of the present line (William the Conqueror) was a Frenchman, and half the peers of England are descendants from the same country; wherefore, by the same method of reasoning, England ought to be governed by France.

Much hath been said of the united strength of Britain and the Colonies, that in conjunction they might bid defiance to the world. But this is mere presumption; the fate of war is uncertain, neither do the expressions mean anything; for this continent would never suffer itself to be drained of inhabitants, to support the British arms in either Asia, Africa, or Europe.

Besides, what have we to do with setting the world at defiance? Our plan is commerce, and that, well attended to, will secure us the peace and friendship of all Europe; because it is the interest of all Europe to have America a free port. Her trade will always be a protection, and her barrenness of gold and silver secure her from invaders.

I challenge the warmest advocate for reconciliation to show a single advantage that this continent can reap by being connected with Great Britain. I repeat the challenge; not a single advantage is derived. Our corn will fetch its price in any market in Europe, and our imported goods must be paid for buy them where we will…

Virginia Declaration of Rights (June 12, 1776)

I That all men are by nature equally free and independent, and have certain inherent rights, of which, when they enter into a state of society, they cannot, by any compact, deprive or divest their posterity; namely, the enjoyment of life and liberty, with the means of acquiring and possessing property, and pursuing and obtaining happiness and safety.

II That all power is vested in, and consequently derived from, the people; that magistrates are their trustees and servants, and at all times amenable to them.

III That government is, or ought to be, instituted for the common benefit, protection, and security of the people, nation or community; of all the various modes and forms of government that is best, which is capable of producing the greatest degree of happiness and safety and is most effectually secured against the danger of maladministration; and that, whenever any government shall be found inadequate or contrary to these purposes, a majority of the community hath an indubitable, unalienable, and indefeasible right to reform, alter or abolish it, in such manner as shall be judged most conducive to the public weal.

IV That no man, or set of men, are entitled to exclusive or separate emoluments or privileges from the community, but in consideration of public services; which, not being descendible, neither ought the offices of magistrate, legislator, or judge be hereditary.

V That the legislative and executive powers of the state should be separate and distinct from the judicative; and, that the members of the two first may be restrained from oppression by feeling and participating the burthens of the people, they should, at fixed periods, be reduced to a private station, return into that body from which they were originally taken, and the vacancies be supplied by frequent, certain, and regular elections in which all, or any part of the former members, to be again eligible, or ineligible, as the laws shall direct.

VI That elections of members to serve as representatives of the people in assembly ought to be free; and that all men, having sufficient evidence of permanent common interest with, and attachment to, the community have the right of suffrage and cannot be taxed or deprived of their property for public uses without their own consent or that of their representatives so elected, nor bound by any law to which they have not, in like manner, assented, for the public good.

VII That all power of suspending laws, or the execution of laws, by any authority without consent of the representatives of the people is injurious to their rights and ought not to be exercised.

VIII That in all capital or criminal prosecutions a man hath a right to demand the cause and nature of his accusation to be confronted with the accusers and witnesses, to call for evidence in his favor, and to a speedy trial by an impartial jury of his vicinage, without whose unanimous consent he cannot be found guilty, nor can he be compelled to give evidence against himself; that no man be deprived of his liberty except by the law of the land or the judgment of his peers.

IX That excessive bail ought not to be required, nor excessive fines imposed; nor cruel and unusual punishments inflicted.

X That general warrants, whereby any officer or messenger may be commanded to search suspected places without evidence of a fact committed, or to seize any person or persons not named, or whose offense is not particularly described and supported by evidence, are grievous and oppressive and ought not to be granted.

XI That in controversies respecting property and in suits between man and man, the ancient trial by jury is preferable to any other and ought to be held sacred.

XII That the freedom of the press is one of the greatest bulwarks of liberty and can never be restrained but by despotic governments.

XIII That a well regulated militia, composed of the body of the people, trained to arms, is the proper, natural, and safe defense of a free state; that standing armies, in time of peace, should be avoided as dangerous to liberty; and that, in all cases, the military should be under strict subordination to, and be governed by, the civil power.

XIV That the people have a right to uniform government; and therefore, that no government separate from, or independent of, the government of Virginia, ought to be erected or established within the limits thereof.

XV That no free government, or the blessings of liberty, can be preserved to any people but by a firm adherence to justice, moderation, temperance, frugality, and virtue and by frequent recurrence to fundamental principles.

XVI That religion, or the duty which we owe to our Creator and the manner of discharging it, can be directed by reason and conviction, not by force or violence; and therefore, all men are equally entitled to the free exercise of religion, according to the dictates of conscience; and that it is the mutual duty of all to practice Christian forbearance, love, and charity towards each other.

Adopted unanimously June 12, 1776 Virginia Convention of Delegates, drafted by Mr. George Mason

The Constitution of Virginia (June 29, 1776)

A declaration of rights made by the representatives of the good people of Virginia, assembled in full and free convention; which rights do pertain to them and their posterity, as the basis and foundation of government.

SEC. 1. That all men are by nature equally free and independent, and have certain inherent rights, of which, when they enter into a state of society, they cannot, by any compact, deprive or divest their posterity, namely, the enjoyment of life and liberty, with the means of acquiring and possessing property, and pursuing and obtaining happiness and safety.

SEC. 2. That all power is vested in, and consequently derived from, the people; that magistrates are their trustees and servants, and at all times amenable to them.

SEC. 3. That government is, or ought to be, instituted for the common benefit, protection, and security of the people, nation, or community; of all the various modes and forms of government, that is best which is capable of producing the greatest degree of happiness and safety, and is most effectually secured against the danger of maladministration; and that, when any government shall be found inadequate or contrary to these purposes, a majority of the community hath an indubitable, inalienable, and indefeasible right to reform, alter, or abolish it, in such manner as shall be judged most conducive to the public weal.

SEC. 4. That no man, or set of men, are entitled to exclusive or separate emoluments or privileges from the community, but in consideration of public services; which, not being descendible, neither ought the offices of magistrate, legislator, or judge to be hereditary.

SEC. 5. That the legislative and executive powers of the State should be separate and distinct from the judiciary; and that the members of the two first may be restrained from oppression, by feeling and participating the burdens of the people, they should, at fixed periods, be reduced to a private station, return into that body from which they were originally taken, and the vacancies be supplied by frequent, certain, and regular elections, in which all, or any part of the former members, to be again eligible, or ineligible, as the laws shall direct.

SEC. 6. That elections of members to serve as representatives of the people, in assembly, ought to be free; and that all men, having sufficient evidence of permanent common interest with, and attachment to, the community, have the right of suffrage, and cannot be taxed or deprived of their property for public uses, without their own consent, or that of their representives so elected, nor bound by any law to which they have not, in like manner, assembled, for the public good.

SEC. 7. That all power of suspending laws, or the execution of laws, by any authority, without consent of the representatives of the people, is injurious to their rights, and ought not to be exercised.

SEC. 8. That in all capital or criminal prosecutions a man bath a right to demand the cause and nature of his accusation, to be confronted with the accusers and witnesses, to call for evidence in his favor, and to a speedy trial by an impartial jury of twelve men of his vicinage, without whose unanimous consent he cannot be found guilty; nor can he be compelled to give evidence against himself; that no man be deprived of his liberty, except by the law of the land or the judgment of his peers.

SEC. 9. That excessive bail ought not to be required, nor excessive fines imposed, nor cruel and unusual punishments inflicted.

SEC. 10. That general warrants, whereby an officer or messenger may be commanded to search suspected places without evidence of a fact committed, or to seize any person or persons not named, or whose offence is not particularly described and supported by evidence, are grievous and oppressive, and ought not to be granted.

SEC. 11. That in controversies respecting property, and in suits between man and man, the ancient trial by jury is preferable to any other, and ought to be held sacred.

SEC. 12. That the freedom of the press is one of the great bulwarks of liberty, and can never be restrained but by despotic governments.

SEC. 13. That a well-regulated militia, composed of the body of the people, trained to arms, is the proper, natural, and safe defence of a free State; that standing armies, in time of peace, should be avoided, as dangerous to liberty; and that in all cases the military should be under strict subordination to, and governed by, the civil power.

SEC. 14. That the people have a right to uniform government; and, therefore, that no government separate from, or independent of the government of Virginia, ought to be erected or established within the limits thereof.

SEC. 15. That no free government, or the blessings of liberty, can be preserved to any people, but by a firm adherence to justice, moderation, temperance, frugality, and virtue, and by frequent recurrence to fundamental principles.

SEC. 16. That religion, or the duty which we owe to our Creator, and the manner of discharging it, can be directed only by reason and conviction, not by force or violence; and therefore all men are equally entitled to the free exercise of religion, according to the dictates of conscience; and that it is the mutual duty of all to practice Christian forbearance, love, and charity towards each other.

Declaration of Independence (July 4, 1776)

When in the course of human events, it becomes necessary for one people to dissolve the political bands which have connected them with another, and to assume among the powers of the earth, the separate and equal station to which the laws of nature and of nature's God entitle them, a decent respect to the opinions of mankind requires that they should declare the causes which impel them to the separation.

We hold these truths to be self-evident:

That all men are created equal; that they are endowed by their Creator with certain unalienable rights; that among these are life, liberty, and the pursuit of happiness; that, to secure these rights, governments are instituted among men, deriving their just powers from the consent of the governed; that whenever any form of government becomes destructive of these ends, it is the right of the people to alter or to abolish it, and to institute new government, laying its foundation on such principles, and organizing its powers in such form, as to them shall seem most likely to effect their safety and happiness.

Prudence, indeed, will dictate that governments long established should not be changed for light and transient causes; and accordingly all experience hath shown that mankind are more disposed to suffer, while evils are sufferable than to right themselves by abolishing the forms to which they are accustomed. But when a long train of abuses and usurpations, pursuing invariably the same object, evinces a design to reduce them under absolute despotism, it is their right, it is their duty, to throw off such government, and to provide new guards for their future security.

Such has been the patient sufferance of these colonies; and such is now the necessity which constrains them to alter their former systems of government. The history of the present King of Great Britain is a history of repeated injuries and usurpations, all having in direct object the establishment of an absolute tyranny over these states. To prove this, let facts be submitted to a candid world.

He has refused his assent to laws, the most wholesome and necessary for the public good.

He has forbidden his governors to pass laws of immediate and pressing importance, unless suspended in their operation till his assent should be obtained; and, when so suspended, he has utterly neglected to attend to them.

He has refused to pass other laws for the accommodation of large districts of people, unless those people would relinquish the right of representation in the legislature, a right inestimable to them, and formidable to tyrants only.

He has called together legislative bodies at places unusual uncomfortable, and distant from the depository of their public records, for the sole purpose of fatiguing them into compliance with his measures.

He has dissolved representative houses repeatedly, for opposing, with manly firmness, his invasions on the rights of the people.

He has refused for a long time, after such dissolutions, to cause others to be elected; whereby the legislative powers, incapable of annihilation, have returned to the people at large for their exercise; the state remaining, in the mean time, exposed to all the dangers of invasions from without and convulsions within.

He has endeavored to prevent the population of these states; for that purpose obstructing the laws for naturalization of foreigners; refusing to pass others to encourage their migration hither, and raising the conditions of new appropriations of lands.

He has obstructed the administration of justice, by refusing his assent to laws for establishing judiciary powers.

He has made judges dependent on his will alone, for the tenure of their offices, and the amount and payment of their salaries.

He has erected a multitude of new offices, and sent hither swarms of officers to harass our people and eat out their substance.

He has kept among us, in times of peace, standing armies, without the consent of our legislatures.

He has affected to render the military independent of, and superior to, the civil power.

He has combined with others to subject us to a jurisdiction foreign to our Constitution and unacknowledged by our laws, giving his assent to their acts of pretended legislation:

For quartering large bodies of armed troops among us;

For protecting them, by a mock trial, from punishment for any murders which they should commit on the inhabitants of these states;

For cutting off our trade with all parts of the world;

For imposing taxes on us without our consent;

For depriving us, in many cases, of the benefits of trial by jury;

For transporting us beyond seas, to be tried for pretended offenses;

For abolishing the free system of English laws in a neighboring province, establishing therein an arbitrary government, and enlarging its boundaries, so as to render it at once an example and fit instrument for introducing the same absolute rule into these colonies;

For taking away our charters, abolishing our most valuable laws, and altering fundamentally the forms of our governments;

For suspending our own legislatures, and declaring themselves invested with power to legislate for us in all cases whatsoever.

He has abdicated government here, by declaring us out of his protection and waging war against us.

He has plundered our seas, ravaged our coasts, burned our towns, and destroyed the lives of our people.

He is at this time transporting large armies of foreign mercenaries to complete the works of death, desolation, and tyranny already begun with circumstances of cruelty and perfidy scarcely paralleled in the most barbarous ages, and totally unworthy the head of a civilized nation.

He has constrained our fellow-citizens, taken captive on the high seas, to bear arms against their country, to become the executioners of their friends and brethren, or to fall themselves by their hands.

He has excited domestic insurrection among us, and has endeavored to bring on the inhabitants of our frontiers the merciless Indian savages, whose known rule of warfare is an undistinguished destruction of all ages, sexes, and conditions.

In every stage of these oppressions we have petitioned for redress in the most humble terms; our repeated petitions have been answered only by repeated injury. A prince, whose character is thus marked by every act which may define a tyrant, is unfit to be the ruler of a free people.

Nor have we been wanting in our attentions to our British brethren. We have warned them, from time to time, of attempts by their legislature to extend an unwarrantable jurisdiction over us. We have reminded them of the circumstances of our emigration and settlement here. We have appealed to their native justice and magnanimity; and we have conjured them, by the ties of our common kindred, to disavow these usurpations which would inevitably interrupt our connections and correspondence. They too, have been deaf to the voice of justice and of consanguinity. We must, therefore, acquiesce in the necessity which denounces our separation, and hold them as we hold the rest of mankind, enemies in war, in peace friends.

We, therefore, the representatives of the United States of America, in General Congress assembled, appealing to the Supreme Judge of the world for the rectitude of our intentions, do, in the name and by the authority of the good people of these colonies solemnly publish and declare, That these United Colonies are, and of right ought to be, *FREE AND INDEPENDENT STATES*; that they are absolved from all allegiance to the British crown and that all political connection between them and the state of Great Britain is, and ought to be, totally dissolved; and that, as free and independent states, they have full power to levy war, conclude peace, contract alliances, establish commerce, and do all other acts and things which independent states may of right do.

And for the support of this declaration, with a firm reliance on the protection of Divine Providence, we mutually pledge to each other our lives, our fortunes, and our sacred honor.

The American Crisis I, Excerpt from (1776)
Pamphlet by Thomas Paine (December 23, 1776)

THESE are the times that try men's souls. The summer soldier and the sunshine patriot will, in this crisis, shrink from the service of their country; but he that stands it now, deserves the love and thanks of man and woman.

Tyranny, like hell, is not easily conquered; yet we have this consolation with us, that the harder the conflict, the more glorious the triumph. What we obtain too cheap, we esteem too lightly: it is dearness only that gives every thing its value.

Heaven knows how to put a proper price upon its goods; and it would be strange indeed if so celestial an article as FREEDOM should not be highly rated. Britain, with an army to enforce her tyranny, has declared that she has a right (not only to TAX) but "to BIND us in ALL CASES WHATSOEVER," and if being bound in that manner, is not slavery, then is there not such a thing as slavery upon earth. Even the expression is impious; for so unlimited a power can belong only to God.

Whether the independence of the continent was declared too soon, or delayed too long, I will not now enter into as an argument; my own simple opinion is, that had it been eight months earlier, it would have been much better. We did not make a proper use of last winter, neither could we, while we were in a dependent state. However, the fault, if it were one, was all our own; we have none to blame but ourselves. But no great deal is lost yet. All that Howe has been doing for this month past, is rather a ravage than a conquest, which the spirit of the Jerseys, a year ago, would have quickly repulsed, and which time and a little resolution will soon recover…

Articles of Confederation
Agreed to by Congress in 1777;
In force after ratification by Maryland in 1781

To all to whom these Presents shall come, we the undersigned Delegates of the States affixed to our Names send greeting.

Articles of Confederation and perpetual Union between the states of New Hampshire, Massachusetts-bay Rhode Island and Providence Plantations, Connecticut, New York, New Jersey, Pennsylvania, Delaware, Maryland, Virginia, North Carolina, South Carolina and Georgia.

I. The Stile of this Confederacy shall be
"The United States of America".

II. Each state retains its sovereignty, freedom, and independence, and every power, jurisdiction, and right, which is not by this Confederation expressly delegated to the United States, in Congress assembled.

III. The said States hereby severally enter into a firm league of friendship with each other, for their common defense, the security of their liberties, and their mutual and general welfare, binding themselves to assist each other, against all force offered to, or attacks made upon them, or any of them, on account of religion, sovereignty, trade, or any other pretense whatever.

IV. The better to secure and perpetuate mutual friendship and intercourse among the people of the different States in this Union, the free inhabitants of each of these States, paupers, vagabonds, and fugitives from justice excepted, shall be entitled to all privileges and immunities of free citizens in the several States; and the people of each State shall free ingress and regress to and from any other State, and shall enjoy therein all the privileges of trade and commerce, subject to the same duties, impositions, and restrictions as the inhabitants thereof respectively, provided that such restrictions shall not extend so far as to prevent the removal of property imported into any State, to any other State, of which the owner is an inhabitant; provided also that no imposition, duties or restriction shall be laid by any State, on the property of the United States, or either of them.

If any person guilty of, or charged with, treason, felony, or other high misdemeanor in any State, shall flee from justice, and be found in any of the United States, he shall, upon demand of the Governor or executive power of the State from which he fled, be delivered up and removed to the State having jurisdiction of his offense.

Full faith and credit shall be given in each of these States to the records, acts, and judicial proceedings of the courts and magistrates of every other State.

V. For the most convenient management of the general interests of the United States, delegates shall be annually appointed in such manner as the legislatures of each State shall direct, to meet in Congress on the first Monday in November, in every year, with a power reserved to each State to recall its delegates, or any of them, at any time within the year, and to send others in their stead for the remainder of the year.

No State shall be represented in Congress by less than two, nor more than seven members; and no person shall be capable of being a delegate for more than three years in any term of six years; nor shall any person, being a delegate, be capable of holding any office under the United States, for which he, or another for his benefit, receives any salary, fees or emolument of any kind.

Each State shall maintain its own delegates in a meeting of the States, and while they act as members of the committee of the States.

In determining questions in the United States in Congress assembled, each State shall have one vote.

Freedom of speech and debate in Congress shall not be impeached or questioned in any court or place out of Congress, and the members of Congress shall be protected in their persons from arrests or imprisonments, during the time of their going to and from, and attendance on Congress, except for treason, felony, or breach of the peace.

VI. No State, without the consent of the United States in Congress assembled, shall send any embassy to, or receive any embassy from, or enter into any conference, agreement, alliance or treaty with any King, Prince or State; nor shall any person holding any office of profit or trust under the United States, or any of them, accept any present, emolument, office or title of any kind whatever from any King, Prince or foreign State; nor shall the United States in Congress assembled, or any of them, grant any title of nobility.

No two or more States shall enter into any treaty, confederation or alliance whatever between them, without the consent of the United States in Congress assembled, specifying accurately the purposes for which the same is to be entered into, and how long it shall continue.

No State shall lay any imposts or duties, which may interfere with any stipulations in treaties, entered into by the United States in Congress assembled, with any King, Prince or State, in pursuance of any treaties already proposed by Congress, to the courts of France and Spain.

No vessel of war shall be kept up in time of peace by any State, except such number only, as shall be deemed necessary by the United States in Congress assembled, for the defense of such State, or its trade; nor shall any body of forces be kept up by any State in time of peace, except such number only, as in the judgment of the United States in Congress assembled, shall be deemed requisite to garrison the forts necessary for the defense of such State; but every State shall always keep up a well-regulated and disciplined militia, sufficiently armed and accoutered, and shall provide and constantly have ready for use, in public stores, a due number of filed pieces and tents, and a proper quantity of arms, ammunition and camp equipage.

No State shall engage in any war without the consent of the United States in Congress assembled, unless such State be actually invaded by enemies, or shall have received certain advice of a resolution being formed by some nation of Indians to invade such State, and the danger is so imminent as not to admit of a delay till the United States in Congress assembled can be consulted; nor shall any State grant commissions to any ships or vessels of war, nor letters of marque or reprisal, except it be after a declaration of war by the United States in Congress assembled, and then only against the Kingdom or State and the subjects thereof, against which war has been so declared, and under such regulations as shall be established by the United States in Congress assembled, unless such State be infested by pirates, in which case vessels of war may be fitted out for that occasion, and kept so long as the danger shall continue, or until the United States in Congress assembled shall determine otherwise.

VII. When land forces are raised by any State for the common defense, all officers of or under the rank of colonel, shall be appointed by the legislature of each State respectively, by whom such forces shall be raised, or in such manner as such State shall direct, and all vacancies shall be filled up by the State which first made the appointment.

VIII. All charges of war, and all other expenses that shall be incurred for the common defense or general welfare, and allowed by the United States in Congress assembled, shall be defrayed out of a common treasury, which shall be supplied by the several States in proportion to the value of all land within each State, granted or surveyed for any person, as such land and the buildings and improvements thereon shall be estimated according to such mode as the United States in Congress assembled, shall from time to time direct and appoint.

The taxes for paying that proportion shall be laid and levied by the authority and direction of the legislatures of the several States within the time agreed upon by the United States in Congress assembled.

IX. The United States in Congress assembled, shall have the sole and exclusive right and power of determining on peace and war, except in the cases mentioned in the sixth article -- of sending and receiving ambassadors -- entering into treaties and alliances, provided that no treaty of commerce shall be made whereby the legislative power of the respective States shall be restrained from imposing such imposts and duties on foreigners, as their own people are subjected to, or from prohibiting the exportation or importation of any species of goods or commodities whatsoever -- of establishing rules for deciding in all cases, what captures on land or water shall be legal, and in what manner prizes taken by land or naval forces in the service of the United States shall be divided or appropriated -- of granting letters of marque and reprisal in times of peace -- appointing courts for the trial of piracies and felonies committed on the high seas and establishing courts for receiving and determining finally appeals in all cases of captures, provided that no member of Congress shall be appointed a judge of any of the said courts.

The United States in Congress assembled shall also be the last resort on appeal in all disputes and differences now subsisting or that hereafter may arise between two or more States concerning boundary, jurisdiction or any other causes whatever; which authority shall always be exercised in the manner following. Whenever the legislative or executive authority or lawful agent of any State in controversy with another shall present a petition to Congress stating the matter in question and praying for a hearing, notice thereof shall be given by order of Congress to the legislative or executive authority of the other State in controversy, and a day assigned for the appearance of the parties by their lawful agents, who shall then be directed to appoint by joint consent, commissioners or judges to constitute a court for hearing and determining the matter in question: but if they cannot agree, Congress shall name three persons out of each of the United States, and from the list of such persons each party shall alternately strike out one, the petitioners beginning, until the number shall be reduced to thirteen; and from that number not less than seven, nor more than nine names as Congress shall direct, shall in the presence of Congress be drawn out by lot, and the persons whose names shall be so drawn or any five of them, shall be commissioners or judges, to hear and finally determine the controversy, so always as a major part of the judges who shall hear the cause shall agree in the determination: and if either party shall neglect to attend at the day appointed, without showing reasons, which Congress shall judge sufficient, or being present shall refuse to strike, the Congress shall proceed to nominate three persons out of each State, and the secretary of Congress shall strike in behalf of such party absent or refusing; and the judgment and sentence of the court to be appointed, in the manner before prescribed, shall be final and conclusive; and if any of the parties shall refuse to submit to the authority of such court, or to appear or defend their claim or cause, the court shall nevertheless proceed to pronounce sentence, or judgment, which shall in like manner be final and decisive, the judgment or sentence and other proceedings being in either case transmitted to Congress, and lodged among the acts of

Congress for the security of the parties concerned: provided that every commissioner, before he sits in judgment, shall take an oath to be administered by one of the judges of the supreme or superior court of the State, where the cause shall be tried, 'well and truly to hear and determine the matter in question, according to the best of his judgment, without favor, affection or hope of reward': provided also, that no State shall be deprived of territory for the benefit of the United States.

All controversies concerning the private right of soil claimed under different grants of two or more States, whose jurisdictions as they may respect such lands, and the States which passed such grants are adjusted, the said grants or either of them being at the same time claimed to have originated antecedent to such settlement of jurisdiction, shall on the petition of either party to the Congress of the United States, be finally determined as near as may be in the same manner as is before prescribed for deciding disputes respecting territorial jurisdiction between different States.

The United States in Congress assembled shall also have the sole and exclusive right and power of regulating the alloy and value of coin struck by their own authority, or by that of the respective States -- fixing the standards of weights and measures throughout the United States -- regulating the trade and managing all affairs with the Indians, not members of any of the States, provided that the legislative right of any State within its own limits be not infringed or violated -- establishing or regulating post offices from one State to another, throughout all the United States, and exacting such postage on the papers passing through the same as may be requisite to defray the expenses of the said office -- appointing all officers of the land forces, in the service of the United States, excepting regimental officers -- appointing all the officers of the naval forces, and commissioning all officers whatever in the service of the United States -- making rules for the government and regulation of the said land and naval forces, and directing their operations.

The United States in Congress assembled shall have authority to appoint a committee, to sit in the recess of Congress, to be denominated 'A Committee of the States', and to consist of one delegate from each State; and to appoint such other committees and civil officers as may be necessary for managing the general affairs of the United States under their direction -- to appoint one of their members to preside, provided that no person be allowed to serve in the office of president more than one year in any term of three years; to ascertain the necessary sums of money to be raised for the service of the United States, and to appropriate and apply the same for defraying the public expenses -- to borrow money, or emit bills on the credit of the United States, transmitting every half-year to the respective States an account of the sums of money so borrowed or emitted -- to build and equip a navy -- to agree upon the number of land forces, and to make requisitions from each State for its quota, in proportion to the number of white inhabitants in such State; which requisition shall be binding, and thereupon the legislature of each State shall appoint the regimental officers, raise the men and cloath, arm and equip them in a solid-like manner, at the expense of the United States; and the officers and men so cloathed, armed and equipped shall march to the place appointed, and within the time agreed on by the United States in Congress assembled. But if the United States in Congress assembled shall, on consideration of circumstances judge proper that any State should not raise men, or should raise a smaller number of men than the quota thereof, such extra number shall be raised, officered, cloathed, armed and equipped in the same manner as the quota of each State, unless the legislature of such State shall judge that such extra number cannot be safely spread out in the same, in which case they shall raise, officer, cloath, arm and equip as many of such extra number as they judeg can be safely spared. And the officers and men so cloathed, armed, and equipped, shall march to the place appointed, and within the time agreed on by the United States in Congress assembled.

The United States in Congress assembled shall never engage in a war, nor grant letters of marque or reprisal in time of peace, nor enter into any treaties or alliances, nor coin money, nor regulate the value thereof, nor ascertain the sums and expenses necessary for the defense and welfare of the United States, or any of them, nor emit bills, nor borrow money on the credit of the United States, nor appropriate money, nor agree upon the number of vessels of war, to be built or purchased, or the number of land or sea forces to be raised, nor appoint a commander in chief of the army or navy, unless nine States assent to the same: nor shall a question on any other point, except for adjourning from day to day be determined, unless by the votes of the majority of the United States in Congress assembled.

The Congress of the United States shall have power to adjourn to any time within the year, and to any place within the United States, so that no period of adjournment be for a longer duration than the space of six months, and shall publish the journal of their proceedings monthly, except such parts thereof relating to treaties, alliances or military operations, as in their judgment require secrecy; and the yeas and nays of the delegates of each State on any question shall be entered on the journal, when it is desired by any delegates of a State, or any of them, at his or their request shall be furnished with a transcript of the said journal, except such parts as are above excepted, to lay before the legislatures of the several States.

X. The Committee of the States, or any nine of them, shall be authorized to execute, in the recess of Congress, such of the powers of Congress as the United States in Congress assembled, by the consent of the nine States, shall from time to time think expedient to vest them with; provided that no power be delegated to the said Committee, for the exercise of which, by the Articles of Confederation, the voice of nine States in the Congress of the United States assembled be requisite.

XI. Canada acceding to this confederation, and adjoining in the measures of the United States, shall be admitted into, and entitled to all the advantages of this Union; but no other colony shall be admitted into the same, unless such admission be agreed to by nine States.

XII. All bills of credit emitted, monies borrowed, and debts contracted by, or under the authority of Congress, before the assembling of the United States, in pursuance of the present confederation, shall be deemed and considered as a charge against the United States, for payment and satisfaction whereof the said United States, and the public faith are hereby solemnly pledged.

XIII. Every State shall abide by the determination of the United States in Congress assembled, on all questions which by this confederation are submitted to them. And the Articles of this Confederation shall be inviolably observed by every State, and the Union shall be perpetual; nor shall any alteration at any time hereafter be made in any of them; unless such alteration be agreed to in a Congress of the United States, and be afterwards confirmed by the legislatures of every State.

And Whereas it hath pleased the Great Governor of the World to incline the hearts of the legislatures we respectively represent in Congress, to approve of, and to authorize us to ratify the said Articles of Confederation and perpetual Union. Know Ye that we the undersigned delegates, by virtue of the power and authority to us given for that purpose, do by these presents, in the name and in behalf of our respective constituents, fully and entirely ratify and confirm each and every of the said Articles of Confederation and perpetual Union, and all and singular the matters and things therein contained: And we do further solemnly plight and engage the faith of our respective constituents, that they shall abide by the determinations of the United States in Congress assembled, on all questions, which by the said Confederation are submitted to them. And that the Articles thereof shall be inviolably observed by the States we respectively represent, and that the Union shall be perpetual.

In Witness whereof we have hereunto set our hands in Congress. Done at Philadelphia in the State of Pennsylvania the ninth day of July in the Year of our Lord One Thousand Seven Hundred and Seventy-Eight, and in the Third Year of the independence of America.

The Northwest Ordinance (1787)

Sec 1. *Be it ordained by the United States in Congress assembled,* That the said territory, for the purposes of temporary government, be one district, subject, however, to be divided into two districts, as future circumstances may, in the opinion of Congress, make it expedient.

Sec 2. *Be it ordained by the authority aforesaid,* That the estates, both of resident and nonresident proprietors in the said territory…

Sec. 3. *Be it ordained by the authority aforesaid,* That there shall be appointed from time to time by Congress, a governor, whose commission shall continue in force for the term of three years, unless sooner revoked by Congress; he shall reside in the district, and have a freehold estate therein in 1,000 acres of land, while in the exercise of his office.

Sec. 4. There shall be appointed from time to time by Congress, a secretary, whose commission shall continue in force for four years unless sooner revoked…

Sec. 5. The governor and judges, or a majority of them, shall adopt and publish in the district such laws of the original States, criminal and civil, as may be necessary and best suited to the circumstances of the district, and report them to Congress from time to time…

Sec. 6. The governor, for the time being, shall be commander in chief of the militia, appoint and commission all officers in the same below the rank of general officers; all general officers shall be appointed and commissioned by Congress.

Sec. 7. Previous to the organization of the general assembly, the governor shall appoint such magistrates and other civil officers in each county or township, as he shall find necessary for the preservation of the peace and good order in the same: After the general assembly shall be organized, the powers and duties of the magistrates and other civil officers shall be regulated and defined by the said assembly; but all magistrates and other civil officers not herein otherwise directed, shall during the continuance of this temporary government, be appointed by the governor.

Sec. 8. For the prevention of crimes and injuries, the laws to be adopted or made shall have force in all parts of the district, and for the execution of process, criminal and civil, the governor shall make proper divisions thereof; and he shall proceed from time to time as circumstances may require, to lay out the parts of the district in which the Indian titles shall have been extinguished, into counties and townships, subject, however, to such alterations as may thereafter be made by the legislature.

Sec. 9. So soon as there shall be five thousand free male inhabitants of full age in the district, upon giving proof thereof to the governor, they shall receive authority, with time and place, to elect a representative from their counties or townships to represent them in the general assembly…

Sec. 10. The representatives thus elected, shall serve for the term of two years…

Sec. 11. The general assembly or legislature shall consist of the governor, legislative council, and a house of representatives. The Legislative Council shall consist of five members, to continue in office five years, unless sooner removed by Congress…

Sec. 12. The governor, judges, legislative council, secretary, and such other officers as Congress shall appoint in the district, shall take an oath or affirmation of fidelity and of office…

Sec. 13. And, for extending the fundamental principles of civil and religious liberty, which form the basis whereon these republics, their laws and constitutions are erected; to fix and establish those principles as the basis of all laws, constitutions, and governments, which forever hereafter shall be formed in the said territory: to provide also for the establishment of States, and permanent government therein, and for their admission to a share in the federal councils on an equal footing with the original States, at as early periods as may be consistent with the general interest:

Sec. 14. It is hereby ordained and declared by the authority aforesaid, That the following articles shall be considered as articles of compact between the original States and the people and States in the said territory and forever remain unalterable, unless by common consent, to wit:

Art. 1. No person, demeaning himself in a peaceable and orderly manner, shall ever be molested on account of his mode of worship or religious sentiments, in the said territory.

Art. 2. The inhabitants of the said territory shall always be entitled to the benefits of the writ of *habeas corpus*, and of the trial by jury; of a proportionate representation of the people in the legislature; and of judicial proceedings according to the course of the common law. All persons shall be bailable, unless for capital offenses, where the proof shall be evident or the presumption great. All fines shall be moderate; and no cruel or unusual punishments shall be inflicted. No man shall be deprived of his liberty or property, but by the judgment of his peers or the law of the land; and, should the public exigencies make it necessary, for the common preservation, to take any person's property, or to demand his particular services, full compensation shall be made for the same. And, in the just preservation of rights and property, it is understood and declared, that no law ought ever to be made, or have force in the said territory, that shall, in any manner whatever, interfere with or affect private contracts or engagements, *bona fide*, and without fraud, previously formed.

Art. 3. Religion, morality, and knowledge, being necessary to good government and the happiness of mankind, schools and the means of education shall forever be encouraged. The utmost good faith shall always be observed towards the Indians; their lands and property shall never be taken from them without their consent; and, in their property, rights, and liberty, they shall never be invaded or disturbed, unless in just and lawful wars authorized by Congress; but laws founded in justice and humanity, shall from time to time be made for preventing wrongs being done to them, and for preserving peace and friendship with them.

Art. 4. The said territory, and the States which may be formed therein, shall forever remain a part of this Confederacy of the United States of America, subject to the Articles of Confederation, and to such alterations therein as shall be constitutionally made; and to all the acts and ordinances of the United States in Congress assembled, conformable thereto.

The inhabitants and settlers in the said territory shall be subject to pay a part of the federal debts contracted or to be contracted, and a proportional part of the expenses of government, to be apportioned on them by Congress according to the same common rule and measure by which apportionments thereof shall be made on the other States; and the taxes for paying their proportion shall be laid and levied by the authority and direction of the legislatures of the district or districts, or new States, as in the original States, within the time agreed upon by the United States in Congress assembled.

The legislatures of those districts or new States, shall never interfere with the primary disposal of the soil by the United States in Congress assembled, nor with any regulations Congress may find necessary for securing the title in such soil to the *bona fide* purchasers. No tax shall be imposed on lands the property of the United States; and, in no case, shall nonresident proprietors be taxed higher than residents. The navigable waters leading into the Mississippi and St. Lawrence, and the carrying places between the same, shall be common highways and forever free, as well to the inhabitants of the said territory as to the citizens of the United States, and those of any other States that may be admitted into the confederacy, without any tax, impost, or duty therefor.

Art. 5. There shall be formed in the said territory, not less than three nor more than five States; and the boundaries of the States…

And, whenever any of the said States shall have sixty thousand free inhabitants therein, such State shall be admitted, by its delegates, into the Congress of the United States, on an equal footing with the original States in all respects whatever, and shall be at liberty to form a permanent constitution and State government:

Provided, the constitution and government so to be formed, shall be republican, and in conformity to the principles contained in these articles; and, so far as it can be consistent with the general interest of the confederacy, such admission shall be allowed at an earlier period, and when there may be a less number of free inhabitants in the State than sixty thousand.

Art. 6. There shall be neither slavery nor involuntary servitude in the said territory, otherwise than in the punishment of crimes whereof the party shall have been duly convicted: *Provided, always,* That any person escaping into the same, from whom labor or service is lawfully claimed in any one of the original States, such fugitive may be lawfully reclaimed and conveyed to the person claiming his or her labor or service as aforesaid.

Be it ordained by the authority aforesaid, That the resolutions of the 23rd of April, 1784, relative to the subject of this ordinance, be, and the same are hereby repealed and declared null and void.

Done by the United States, in Congress assembled, the 13th day of July, in the year of our Lord 1787, and of their soveriegnty and independence the twelfth.

The Federalist Papers : No. 10 (Nov 23, 1787)

The Same Subject Continued:
The Union as a Safeguard Against Domestic Faction and Insurrection

To the People of the State of New York:

AMONG the numerous advantages promised by a well constructed Union, none deserves to be more accurately developed than its tendency to break and control the violence of faction. The friend of popular governments never finds himself so much alarmed for their character and fate, as when he contemplates their propensity to this dangerous vice. He will not fail, therefore, to set a due value on any plan which, without violating the principles to which he is attached, provides a proper cure for it.

The instability, injustice, and confusion introduced into the public councils, have, in truth, been the mortal diseases under which popular governments have everywhere perished; as they continue to be the favorite and fruitful topics from which the adversaries to liberty derive their most specious declamations.

The valuable improvements made by the American constitutions on the popular models, both ancient and modern, cannot certainly be too much admired; but it would be an unwarrantable partiality, to contend that they have as effectually obviated the danger on this side, as was wished and expected.

Complaints are everywhere heard from our most considerate and virtuous citizens, equally the friends of public and private faith, and of public and personal liberty, that our governments are too unstable, that the public good is disregarded in the conflicts of rival parties, and that measures are too often decided, not according to the rules of justice and the rights of the minor party, but by the superior force of an interested and overbearing majority.

However anxiously we may wish that these complaints had no foundation, the evidence, of known facts will not permit us to deny that they are in some degree true. It will be found, indeed, on a candid review of our situation, that some of the distresses under which we labor have been erroneously charged on the operation of our governments; but it will be found, at the same time, that other causes will not alone account for many of our heaviest misfortunes; and, particularly, for that prevailing and increasing distrust of public engagements, and alarm for private rights, which are echoed from one end of the continent to the other. These must be chiefly, if not wholly, effects of the unsteadiness and injustice with which a factious spirit has tainted our public administrations.

By a faction, I understand a number of citizens, whether amounting to a majority or a minority of the whole, who are united and actuated by some common impulse of passion, or of interest, adversed to the rights of other citizens, or to the permanent and aggregate interests of the community.

There are two methods of curing the mischiefs of faction: the one, by removing its causes; the other, by controlling its effects.

There are again two methods of removing the causes of faction: the one, by destroying the liberty which is essential to its existence; the other, by giving to every citizen the same opinions, the same passions, and the same interests.

It could never be more truly said than of the first remedy, that it was worse than the disease. Liberty is to faction what air is to fire, an aliment without which it instantly expires. But it could not be less folly to abolish liberty, which is essential to political life, because it nourishes faction, than it would be to wish the annihilation of air, which is essential to animal life, because it imparts to fire its destructive agency.

The second expedient is as impracticable as the first would be unwise. As long as the reason of man continues fallible, and he is at liberty to exercise it, different opinions will be formed. As long as the connection subsists between his reason and his self-love, his opinions and his passions will have a reciprocal influence on each other; and the former will be objects to which the latter will attach themselves. The diversity in the faculties of men, from which the rights of property originate, is not less an insuperable obstacle to a uniformity of interests. The protection of these faculties is the first object of government. From the protection of different and unequal faculties of acquiring property, the possession of different degrees and kinds of property immediately results; and from the influence of these on the sentiments and views of the respective proprietors, ensues a division of the society into different interests and parties.

The latent causes of faction are thus sown in the nature of man; and we see them everywhere brought into different degrees of activity, according to the different circumstances of civil society. A zeal for different opinions concerning religion, concerning government, and many other points, as well of speculation as of practice; an attachment to different leaders ambitiously contending for pre-eminence and power; or to persons of other descriptions whose fortunes have been interesting to the human passions, have, in turn, divided mankind into parties, inflamed them with mutual animosity, and rendered them much more disposed to vex and oppress each other than to co-operate for their common good. So strong is this propensity of mankind to fall into mutual animosities, that where no substantial occasion presents itself, the most frivolous and fanciful distinctions have been sufficient to kindle their unfriendly passions and excite their most violent conflicts.

But the most common and durable source of factions has been the various and unequal distribution of property. Those who hold and those who are without property have ever formed distinct interests in society. Those who are creditors, and those who are debtors, fall under a like discrimination. A landed interest, a manufacturing interest, a mercantile interest, a moneyed interest, with many lesser interests, grow up of necessity in civilized nations, and divide them into different classes, actuated by different sentiments and views. The regulation of these various and interfering interests forms the principal task of modern legislation, and involves the spirit of party and faction in the necessary and ordinary operations of the government.

No man is allowed to be a judge in his own cause, because his interest would certainly bias his judgment, and, not improbably, corrupt his integrity. With equal, nay with greater reason, a body of men are unfit to be both judges and parties at the same time; yet what are many of the most important acts of legislation, but so many judicial determinations, not indeed concerning the rights of single persons, but concerning the rights of large bodies of citizens?

And what are the different classes of legislators but advocates and parties to the causes which they determine? Is a law proposed concerning private debts? It is a question to which the creditors are parties on one side and the debtors on the other. Justice ought to hold the balance between them.

Yet the parties are, and must be, themselves the judges; and the most numerous party, or, in other words, the most powerful faction must be expected to prevail. Shall domestic manufactures be encouraged, and in what degree, by restrictions on foreign manufactures? are questions which would be differently decided by the landed and the manufacturing classes, and probably by neither with a sole regard to justice and the public good.

The apportionment of taxes on the various descriptions of property is an act which seems to require the most exact impartiality; yet there is, perhaps, no legislative act in which greater opportunity and temptation are given to a predominant party to trample on the rules of justice. Every shilling with which they overburden the inferior number, is a shilling saved to their own pockets.

It is in vain to say that enlightened statesmen will be able to adjust these clashing interests, and render them all subservient to the public good. Enlightened statesmen will not always be at the helm. Nor, in many cases, can such an adjustment be made at all without taking into view indirect and remote considerations, which will rarely prevail over the immediate interest which one party may find in disregarding the rights of another or the good of the whole.

The inference to which we are brought is, that the **causes** of faction cannot be removed, and that relief is only to be sought in the means of controlling its **effects**.

If a faction consists of less than a majority, relief is supplied by the republican principle, which enables the majority to defeat its sinister views by regular vote. It may clog the administration, it may convulse the society; but it will be unable to execute and mask its violence under the forms of the Constitution.

When a majority is included in a faction, the form of popular government, on the other hand, enables it to sacrifice to its ruling passion or interest both the public good and the rights of other citizens. To secure the public good and private rights against the danger of such a faction, and at the same time to preserve the spirit and the form of popular government, is then the great object to which our inquiries are directed. Let me add that it is the great desideratum by which this form of government can be rescued from the opprobrium under which it has so long labored, and be recommended to the esteem and adoption of mankind.

By what means is this object attainable? Evidently by one of two only. Either the existence of the same passion or interest in a majority at the same time must be prevented, or the majority, having such coexistent passion or interest, must be rendered, by their number and local situation, unable to concert and carry into effect schemes of oppression. If the impulse and the opportunity be suffered to coincide, we well know that neither moral nor religious motives can be relied on as an adequate control. They are not found to be such on the injustice and violence of individuals, and lose their efficacy in proportion to the number combined together, that is, in proportion as their efficacy becomes needful.

From this view of the subject it may be concluded that a pure democracy, by which I mean a society consisting of a small number of citizens, who assemble and administer the government in person, can admit of no cure for the mischiefs of faction. A common passion or interest will, in almost every case, be felt by a majority of the whole; a communication and concert result from the form of government itself; and there is nothing to check the inducements to sacrifice the weaker party or an obnoxious individual.

Hence it is that such democracies have ever been spectacles of turbulence and contention; have ever been found incompatible with personal security or the rights of property; and have in general been as short in their lives as they have been violent in their deaths. Theoretic politicians, who have patronized this species of government, have erroneously supposed that by reducing mankind to a perfect equality in their political rights, they would, at the same time, be perfectly equalized and assimilated in their possessions, their opinions, and their passions.

A republic, by which I mean a government in which the scheme of representation takes place, opens a different prospect, and promises the cure for which we are seeking. Let us examine the points in which it varies from pure democracy, and we shall comprehend both the nature of the cure and the efficacy which it must derive from the Union.

The two great points of difference between a democracy and a republic are: first, the delegation of the government, in the latter, to a small number of citizens elected by the rest; secondly, the greater number of citizens, and greater sphere of country, over which the latter may be extended.

The effect of the first difference is, on the one hand, to refine and enlarge the public views, by passing them through the medium of a chosen body of citizens, whose wisdom may best discern the true interest of their country, and whose patriotism and love of justice will be least likely to sacrifice it to temporary or partial considerations. Under such a regulation, it may well happen that the public voice, pronounced by the representatives of the people, will be more consonant to the public good than if pronounced by the people themselves, convened for the purpose.

On the other hand, the effect may be inverted. Men of factious tempers, of local prejudices, or of sinister designs, may, by intrigue, by corruption, or by other means, first obtain the suffrages, and then betray the interests, of the people. The question resulting is, whether small or extensive republics are more favorable to the election of proper guardians of the public weal; and it is clearly decided in favor of the latter by two obvious considerations:

In the first place, it is to be remarked that, however small the republic may be, the representatives must be raised to a certain number, in order to guard against the cabals of a few; and that, however large it may be, they must be limited to a certain number, in order to guard against the confusion of a multitude. Hence, the number of representatives in the two cases not being in proportion to that of the two constituents, and being proportionally greater in the small republic, it follows that, if the proportion of fit characters be not less in the large than in the small republic, the former will present a greater option, and consequently a greater probability of a fit choice.

In the next place, as each representative will be chosen by a greater number of citizens in the large than in the small republic, it will be more difficult for unworthy candidates to practice with success the vicious arts by which elections are too often carried; and the suffrages of the people being more free, will be more likely to centre in men who possess the most attractive merit and the most diffusive and established characters.

It must be confessed that in this, as in most other cases, there is a mean, on both sides of which inconveniences will be found to lie. By enlarging too much the number of electors, you render the representatives too little acquainted with all their local circumstances and lesser interests; as by reducing it too much, you render him unduly attached to these, and too little fit to comprehend and pursue great and national objects. The federal Constitution forms a happy combination in this respect; the great and aggregate interests being referred to the national, the local and particular to the State legislatures.

The other point of difference is, the greater number of citizens and extent of territory which may be brought within the compass of republican than of democratic government; and it is this circumstance principally which renders factious combinations less to be dreaded in the former than in the latter.

The smaller the society, the fewer probably will be the distinct parties and interests composing it; the fewer the distinct parties and interests, the more frequently will a majority be found of the same party; and the smaller the number of individuals composing a majority, and the smaller the compass within which they are placed, the more easily will they concert and execute their plans of oppression.

Extend the sphere, and you take in a greater variety of parties and interests; you make it less probable that a majority of the whole will have a common motive to invade the rights of other citizens; or if such a common motive exists, it will be more difficult for all who feel it to discover their own strength, and to act in unison with each other. Besides other impediments, it may be remarked that, where there is a consciousness of unjust or dishonorable purposes, communication is always checked by distrust in proportion to the number whose concurrence is necessary.

Hence, it clearly appears, that the same advantage which a republic has over a democracy, in controlling the effects of faction, is enjoyed by a large over a small republic,--is enjoyed by the Union over the States composing it. Does the advantage consist in the substitution of representatives whose enlightened views and virtuous sentiments render them superior to local prejudices and schemes of injustice? It will not be denied that the representation of the Union will be most likely to possess these requisite endowments. Does it consist in the greater security afforded by a greater variety of parties, against the event of any one party being able to outnumber and oppress the rest? In an equal degree does the increased variety of parties comprised within the Union, increase this security. Does it, in fine, consist in the greater obstacles opposed to the concert and accomplishment of the secret wishes of an unjust and interested majority? Here, again, the extent of the Union gives it the most palpable advantage.

The influence of factious leaders may kindle a flame within their particular States, but will be unable to spread a general conflagration through the other States. A religious sect may degenerate into a political faction in a part of the Confederacy; but the variety of sects dispersed over the entire face of it must secure the national councils against any danger from that source. A rage for paper money, for an abolition of debts, for an equal division of property, or for any other improper or wicked project, will be less apt to pervade the whole body of the Union than a particular member of it; in the same proportion as such a malady is more likely to taint a particular county or district, than an entire State.

In the extent and proper structure of the Union, therefore, we behold a republican remedy for the diseases most incident to republican government. And according to the degree of pleasure and pride we feel in being republicans, ought to be our zeal in cherishing the spirit and supporting the character of Federalists.

PUBLIUS.

The Danbury Baptist Association, *concerned about religious liberty versus persecution (because they were not part of the Congregationalist establishment in Connecticut),* **wrote to President Thomas Jefferson,** *third president of the new United States.*

October 7, 1801

"Sir, Among the many millions in America and Europe who rejoice in your Election to office; we embrace the first opportunity which we have enjoyed in our collective capacity, since your Inauguration, to express our great satisfaction, in your appointment to the chief Magistracy in the United States; And though our mode of expression may be less courtly and pompous than what many others clothe their addresses with, we beg you, Sir to believe, that none are more sincere.

Our Sentiments are uniformly on the side of Religious Liberty -- That Religion is at all times and places a matter between God and individuals -- That no man ought to suffer in name, person, or effects on account of his religious Opinions - That the legitimate Power of civil government extends no further than to punish the man who works *ill to his neighbor.*

But Sir our constitution of government is not specific. Our ancient charter together with the Laws made coincident therewith, were adopted on the Basis of our government, at the time of our revolution; and such had been our Laws & usages, and such still are; that Religion is considered as the first object of Legislation; and therefore what religious privileges we enjoy (as a minor part of the State) we enjoy as favors granted, and not as inalienable rights: and these favors we receive at the expense of such degrading acknowledgements, as are inconsistent with the rights of freemen. It is not to be wondered at therefore; if those, who seek after power & gain under the pretense of *government & Religion* should reproach their fellow men -- should reproach their chief Magistrate, as an enemy of religion Law & good order because he will not, dare not assume the prerogatives of Jehovah and make Laws to govern the Kingdom of Christ. Sir, we are sensible that the President of the United States, is not the national legislator, and also sensible that the national government cannot destroy the Laws of each State; but our hopes are strong that the sentiments of our beloved

President, which have had such genial affect already, like the radiant beams of the Sun, will shine and prevail through all these States and all the world till Hierarchy and Tyranny be destroyed from the Earth. Sir, when we reflect on your past services, and see a glow of philanthropy and good will shining forth in a course of more than thirty years we have reason to believe that America's God has raised you up to fill the chair of State out of that good will which he bears to the Millions which you preside over. May God strengthen you for the arduous task which providence & the voice of the people have cald you to sustain and support you in your Administration against all the predetermined opposition of those who wish to rise to wealth & importance on the poverty and subjection of the people.

And may the Lord preserve you safe from every evil and bring you at last to his Heavenly Kingdom through Jesus Christ our Glorious Mediator.

Signed in behalf of the Association.
Nehh Dodge
Ephram Robbins
The Committee
Stephen S. Nelson

Thomas Jefferson wrote, in response to the letter from the Danbury Baptist Association: January 1, 1802

Gentlemen:

The affectionate sentiments of esteem and approbation which are so good to express towards me, on behalf of the Danbury Baptist Association, give me the highest satisfaction. My duties dictate a faithful and zealous pursuit of the interests of my constituents, and in proportion as they are persuaded of my fidelity to those duties, the discharge of them becomes more and more pleasing.

Believing with you that religion is a matter which lies solely between man and his God; that he owes account to none other for his faith or his worship; that the legislative powers of the government reach actions only, and not opinions, I contemplate with sovereign reverence that act of the whole American people which declared that their legislature should 'make no law respecting an establishment of religion, or prohibiting the free exercise thereof," thus building a wall of separation between church and State. Adhering to this expression of the supreme will of the nation in behalf of the rights of conscience, I shall see with sincere satisfaction the progress of those sentiments which tend to restore man to all of his natural rights, convinced he has no natural right in opposition to his social duties.

I reciprocate your kind prayers for the protection and blessings of the common Father and Creator of man, and tender you and your religious association, assurances of my high respect and esteem.

Thomas Jefferson

Activities for Before and After Studying the Constitution

Use as few or as many of the following activities as fits your schedule/desires.

I heard someone on a talk radio show who had done the following "survey" at a Rally. I did it with my family members who were home at the time, and with my class. It was interesting to see the reactions to it. I recommend doing it before you teach about the Constitution, to see how many students at least recognize the first 10 amendments of the Constitution.

I've also included a couple of quizzes that I've given at various times in teaching a Constitution Class, sometimes as a Pre-test, but generally as a Post-test. Feel free to modify them to best fit your needs.

The Word Searches can be easily done before a class, and introduction to the terms, etc. The Crossword Puzzles would generally be easier after a set of classes on the Constitution.

Quiz on the Constitution

1: How many amendments are in the "Bill of Rights"? _____

2: How many articles are in the Constitution? _____

3: What does Article 1 cover? _____
_____

4: How many amendments are in the Constitution? _____

5: Who has the right to veto bills? _____

6: What are the two houses of Congress? _____
_____

7: Which branch of government is in control of the military? _____
_____

8: What are the requirements to be a representative? _____
_____

9: What are the requirements to be a senator? _____
_____

10: What are the responsibilities of Congress? _____
_____

Pre-Constitution Word Search

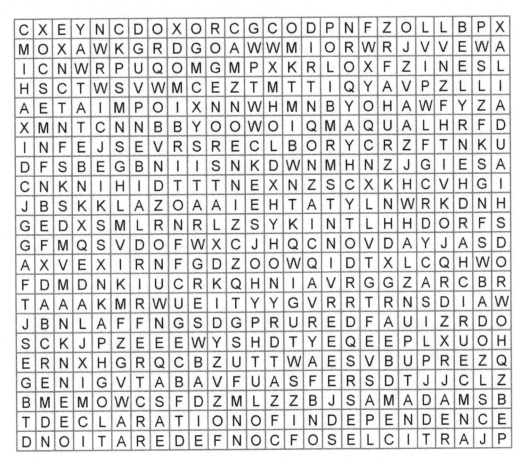

COMMON SENSE
BILL OF RIGHTS
CONTINENTAL CONGRESS
JAMES MADISON
BRITISH WAR DEBT

LAWYER
DECLARATION OF INDEPENDENCE
LEXINGTON AND CONCORD
ARTICLES OF CONFEDERATION
PATRICK HENRY

RICHARD HENRY LEE
BENJAMIN FRANKLIN
SAM ADAMS
NORTHWEST ORDINANCE

Name: _____ Date: _____

Pre-Constitution Word Search

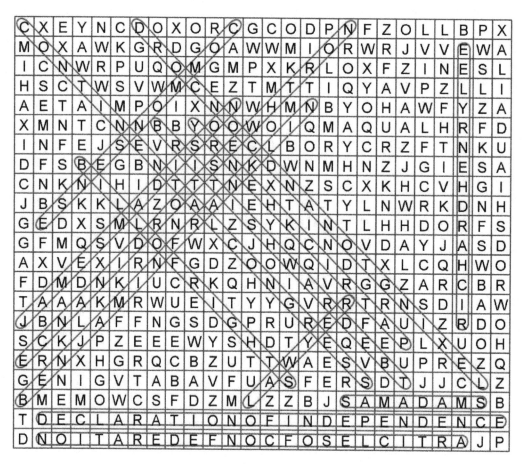

COMMON SENSE
BILL OF RIGHTS
CONTINENTAL CONGRESS
JAMES MADISON
BRITISH WAR DEBT

LAWYER
DECLARATION OF INDEPENDENCE
LEXINGTON AND CONCORD
ARTICLES OF CONFEDERATION
PATRICK HENRY

RICHARD HENRY LEE
BENJAMIN FRANKLIN
SAM ADAMS
NORTHWEST ORDINANCE

Name: _____ Date: _____

Pre-Constitution Matching

1. _____ Oldest delegate at the Constitutional Convention.

2. _____ Important document prepared by Thomas Jefferson during the War.

3. _____ 1787 law establsihed for treatment of new states.

4. _____ "Father" of the Constitution.

5. _____ Primary reason for increased taxes on colonists in 1763.

6. _____ First "great" American Politician.

7. _____ 1785 law establishing how government would divide and sell its new land.

8. _____ Which side slaves fought on during the Revolutionary War.

9. _____ First battles of the Revolutionary War.

10. _____ Document that guided America during and right after the War.

11. _____ First 10 amnedments to the Constitution.

12. _____ Essays written by Hamilton, Madison, and Jay arguing for ratification of the Constitution.

13. _____ Primary occupation of most of the delegates to Convention.

14. _____ Delegate that prepared the resolution that these colonies "ought to be free and independent states."

15. _____ Thomas Paine's electrifying pamphlet that fueled the flames of the Revolution.

16. _____ Official group that guided America during the War.

17. _____ Virginian who refused to attend the Constitutional Convention as a delegate.

1. PATRICK HENRY
2. BOTH
3. ARTICLES OF CONFEDERATION
4. LAWYER
5. NORTHWEST ORDINANCE
6. LEXINGTON AND CONCORD
7. BILL OF RIGHTS
8. LAND ORDINANCE
9. JAMES MADISON
10. RICHARD HENRY LEE
11. FEDERALIST PAPERS
12. CONTINENTAL CONGRESS
13. DECLARATION OF INDEPENDENCE
14. BENJAMIN FRANKLIN
15. BRITISH WAR DEBT
16. SAM ADAMS
17. COMMON SENSE

Name: _____ Date: _____

Pre-Constitution Matching

1. _BENJAMIN FRANKLIN_ — Oldest delegate at the Constitutional Convention.

2. _DECLARATION OF INDEPENDENCE_ — Important document prepared by Thomas Jefferson during the War.

3. _NORTHWEST ORDINANCE_ — 1787 law establsihed for treatment of new states.

4. _JAMES MADISON_ — "Father" of the Constitution.

5. _BRITISH WAR DEBT_ — Primary reason for increased taxes on colonists in 1763.

6. _SAM ADAMS_ — First "great" American Politician.

7. _LAND ORDINANCE_ — 1785 law establishing how government would divide and sell its new land.

8. _BOTH_ — Which side slaves fought on during the Revolutionary War.

9. _LEXINGTON AND CONCORD_ — First battles of the Revolutionary War.

10. _ARTICLES OF CONFEDERATION_ — Document that guided America during and right after the War.

11. _BILL OF RIGHTS_ — First 10 amnedments to the Constitution.

12. _FEDERALIST PAPERS_ — Essays written by Hamilton, Madison, and Jay arguing for ratification of the Constitution.

13. _LAWYER_ — Primary occupation of most of the delegates to Convention.

14. _RICHARD HENRY LEE_ — Delegate that prepared the resolution that these colonies "ought to be free and independent states."

15. _COMMON SENSE_ — Thomas Paine's electrifying pamphlet that fueled the flames of the Revolution.

16. _CONTINENTAL CONGRESS_ — Official group that guided America during the War.

17. _PATRICK HENRY_ — Virginian who refused to attend the Constitutional Convention as a delegate.

---

1. PATRICK HENRY
2. BOTH
3. ARTICLES OF CONFEDERATION
4. LAWYER
5. NORTHWEST ORDINANCE
6. LEXINGTON AND CONCORD
7. BILL OF RIGHTS
8. LAND ORDINANCE
9. JAMES MADISON
10. RICHARD HENRY LEE
11. FEDERALIST PAPERS
12. CONTINENTAL CONGRESS
13. DECLARATION OF INDEPENDENCE
14. BENJAMIN FRANKLIN
15. BRITISH WAR DEBT
16. SAM ADAMS
17. COMMON SENSE

Name: _____ Date: _____

Constitution Word Search

L	X	F	Q	U	B	I	L	L	O	F	R	I	G	H	T	S
O	I	A	M	F	S	I	O	D	P	R	P	H	P	N	V	L
U	Q	W	N	L	D	D	N	A	T	H	I	G	M	D	X	L
J	I	V	F	Q	P	R	E	A	M	B	L	E	E	Y	J	W
K	H	B	W	V	K	7	E	L	C	I	T	R	A	B	D	K
1	S	T	N	E	M	D	N	E	M	A	F	O	T	S	E	R
E	A	Q	O	G	K	Z	Z	A	D	W	D	C	K	Q	O	A
L	Y	R	W	S	G	P	Z	4	J	M	I	V	X	Y	R	B
C	N	N	T	F	D	R	Z	I	E	P	D	G	R	T	I	B
I	M	D	R	I	D	F	M	I	C	L	S	C	I	K	N	W
T	A	R	T	I	C	L	E	3	S	R	C	C	U	A	P	G
R	L	D	C	I	Q	L	K	B	K	W	L	I	U	W	J	C
A	B	N	H	X	Z	A	E	G	B	E	U	A	T	F	I	U
V	O	J	N	H	P	E	R	6	5	L	J	J	V	R	A	T
D	Z	J	T	G	2	E	L	C	I	T	R	A	M	O	A	E

1. Executive Department
2. Judicial Department
3. Amending the Constitution
4. States and their relation to each other
5. Legislative Department
6. Amendments 11 - 27
7. General Provisions
8. Ratification Process
9. First 10 Amendments
10. Statement of Purpose

Name: _____ Date: _____

Constitution Word Search

L	X	F	Q	U	B	I	L	L	O	F	R	I	G	H	T	S
O	I	A	M	F	S	I	O	D	P	R	P	H	P	N	V	L
U	Q	W	N	L	D	D	N	A	T	H	I	G	M	D	X	L
J	I	V	F	Q	P	R	E	A	M	B	L	E	E	Y	J	W
K	H	B	W	V	K	7	E	L	C	I	T	R	A	B	D	K
1	S	T	N	E	M	D	N	E	M	A	F	O	T	S	E	R
E	A	Q	O	G	K	Z	Z	A	D	W	D	C	K	Q	O	A
L	Y	R	W	S	G	P	Z	4	J	M	I	V	X	Y	R	B
C	N	N	T	F	D	R	Z	I	E	P	D	G	R	T	I	B
I	M	D	R	I	D	F	M	I	C	L	S	C	I	K	N	W
T	A	R	T	I	C	L	E	3	S	R	C	C	U	A	P	G
R	L	D	C	I	Q	L	K	B	K	W	L	I	U	W	J	C
A	B	N	H	X	Z	A	E	G	B	E	U	A	T	F	I	U
V	O	J	N	H	P	E	R	6	5	L	J	J	V	R	A	T
D	Z	J	T	G	2	E	L	C	I	T	R	A	M	O	A	E

1. Executive Department
2. Judicial Department
3. Amending the Constitution
4. States and their relation to each other
5. Legislative Department
6. Amendments 11 - 27
7. General Provisions
8. Ratification Process
9. First 10 Amendments
10. Statement of Purpose

Name: _____   Date: _____

Constitution Matching

1. _____ Statement of Purpose

2. _____ Ratification Process

3. _____ Amending the Constitution

4. _____ Legislative Department

5. _____ Judicial Department

6. _____ First 10 Amendments

7. _____ Amendments 11 - 27

8. _____ States and their relation to each other

9. _____ General Provisions

10. _____ Executive Department

1. REST OF AMENDMENTS
2. ARTICLE 1
3. ARTICLE 4
4. BILL OF RIGHTS
5. ARTICLE 7
6. ARTICLE 2
7. ARTICLE 6
8. ARTICLE 3
9. ARTICLE 5
10. PREAMBLE

Name: _____ Date: _____

Constitution Matching

1. _PREAMBLE_____ Statement of Purpose

2. _ARTICLE 7_____ Ratification Process

3. _ARTICLE 5_____ Amending the Constitution

4. _ARTICLE 1_____ Legislative Department

5. _ARTICLE 3_____ Judicial Department

6. _BILL OF RIGHTS_____ First 10 Amendments

7. _REST OF AMENDMENTS___ Amendments 11 - 27

8. _ARTICLE 4_____ States and their relation to each other

9. _ARTICLE 6_____ General Provisions

10. _ARTICLE 2_____ Executive Department

1. REST OF AMENDMENTS
2. ARTICLE 1
3. ARTICLE 4
4. BILL OF RIGHTS
5. ARTICLE 7
6. ARTICLE 2
7. ARTICLE 6
8. ARTICLE 3
9. ARTICLE 5
10. PREAMBLE

Constitution Crossword

ACROSS
2. First 10 Amendments
6. Judicial Department
7. General Provisions
8. States and their relation to each other
9. Amending the Constitution
10. Amendments 11 - 27

DOWN
1. Executive Department
3. Statement of Purpose
4. Ratification Process
5. Legislative Department

REST OF AMENDMENTS	ARTICLE 7
BILL OF RIGHTS	ARTICLE 2
ARTICLE 4	ARTICLE 3
ARTICLE 6	PREAMBLE
ARTICLE 1	ARTICLE 5

Name: _____   Date: _____

Constitution Crossword

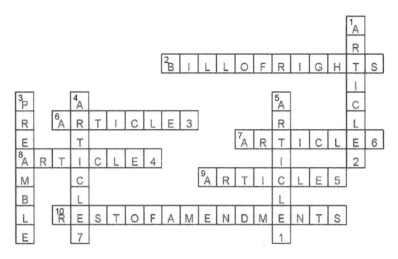

ACROSS
2. First 10 Amendments
6. Judicial Department
7. General Provisions
8. States and their relation to each other
9. Amending the Constitution
10. Amendments 11 - 27

DOWN
1. Executive Department
3. Statement of Purpose
4. Ratification Process
5. Legislative Department

REST OF AMENDMENTS	ARTICLE 7
BILL OF RIGHTS	ARTICLE 2
ARTICLE 4	ARTICLE 3
ARTICLE 6	PREAMBLE
ARTICLE 1	ARTICLE 5

Review of the Writing/Passing of the Constitution

What were the Articles of Confederation? _____

What was the biggest problem under the Articles of Confederation?
_____

Where was the Convention held? _____

What had been done there previously? _____

What was the Convention called after the fact? _____
_____

When was the Convention held? _____

Who were two of the most famous delegates at the convention?
_____

Who took great notes at the convention? _____

Why is he often called "the Father of the Constitution"? _____
_____

When were those notes allowed to be published? _____

How many states sent delegates? _____

Review of the Constitution, page 2

Who didn't, and why?
_____

How many delegates were at the convention altogether? _____

What was the original reason for the convention?
_____

What was the first plan proposed at the Convention? _____

Who favored this plan? _____

What was the next plan proposed? _____

Who favored it? _____

Who "saved the day" at this point? _____

What did he do? _____
_____

What was the "Three-Fifths Compromise"? _____

Did all the delegates sign the Constitution when it was finished? _____

Review of the Constitution, page 3

Was it a "unanimous" decision? _____

Why or why not? _____

What was Alexander Hamilton's position on the finished document?
_____

What was the next step for the Constitution? _____
_____

Who supported the Constitution more, the Federalists or the anti-Federalists?
_____

What was missing from the original Constitution? _____

Which state ratified the Constitution first? _____

How many states had to ratify it for it to become "the law of the Land"? _____

When did that happen? _____

Notes:

Made in the USA
Columbia, SC
01 July 2019